To my parents, Terry and Alan,
who have given me the world.

1ST
EDITION
VERY
RARE

THIS EDITION CONTAINS MINUSCULE
ERRORS WHICH HAVE SINCE
BEEN AMENDED. IT WILL
NEVER BE PRINTED
AGAIN.

GET AWAY!

DESIGN YOUR IDEAL TRIP, TRAVEL WITH EASE, AND RECLAIM YOUR FREEDOM

DAVID AXELROD

The information presented herein represents the views of the author as of the date of publication. This book is presented for informational purposes only. Due to the rate at which conditions change, the author reserves the right to alter and update his opinions based on new conditions. While every attempt has been made to verify the information in this book, neither the author nor his affiliates/partners assume any responsibility for errors, inaccuracies, or omissions.

LIONCREST
PUBLISHING

GET AWAY!
Design Your Ideal Trip, Travel with Ease, and Reclaim Your Freedom

ISBN HARDCOVER: 978-1-5445-2549-5
    PAPERBACK: 978-1-5445-2547-1
    EBOOK: 978-1-5445-2548-8
    AUDIOBOOK: 978-1-5445-2741-3

In me there are two souls, alas, and their

Division tears my life in two.

One loves the world, it clutches her, it binds

Itself to her, clinging with furious lust;

The other longs to soar beyond the dust

Into the realm of high ancestral minds.

Are there no spirits moving in the air,

Ruling the region between earth and sky?

Come down then to me from your golden mists on high,

And to new, many-coloured life, oh take me there!

Give me a magic cloak to carry me

Away to some far place, some land untold,

And I'd not part with it for silk or gold

Or a king's crown, so precious it would be!

—GOETHE, *Faust*

CONTENTS

INTRODUCTION

When I dropped out of law school six weeks into my first semester, I didn't have a clue what I would do next.

I have nothing against the legal profession. I just don't belong in it. So I made it my mission to reclaim my freedom and become who I've always been: an inimitable creative devoted to travel.

I've always been a traveler. The bug bit early, thanks to my wander-loving parents. When I first visited Hong Kong, it was still a British colony. I spent school breaks in Kenya, Morocco, and Vietnam and teenage summers on homestays in Cuba and Chile. I saw Machu Picchu, the Taj Mahal, and the Great Wall of China before I graduated college.

I have now visited over fifty countries and all seven continents for leisure and on assignment as a travel writer and photographer. I've covered everything from the bizarre extravagance of Dubai to the charming quagmire that is Newfoundland. On my favorite gig as an adventure documentarian, a major paint conglomerate made me their social media spokesman and tasked me with inventing an original paint palette. (Long story short, you can now buy a five-gallon bucket of Mermaid Tears at Home Depot.)

I've always been a storyteller. Travel nurtured the knack. Without sharing true stories about my adventures (and misadventures), I felt

1

lonely and frustrated. I wanted friends to understand not just that I went somewhere but that going there broadened my perspective. If I could show them how, I could broaden their perspective by proxy. Stories turned my travel experiences into gifts that I could give to others, rather than hoarding for myself. Telling them now feels even better than living them.

I've always been an optimist. I named my travel brand 2STRAWS because the metaphor represents everything I love about exploration and life itself—the drinking-in and sharing of all the beauty and wonder that earth has to offer. Two straws (100 percent compostable) stand tall, in a delectable but not-too-sugary beverage, for the good life we all deserve. Go on, have a sip.

I have reclaimed my freedom, but I won't be satisfied until you reclaim yours, too. You had it as a child, but like water, it's hard to hold. Society did its societal thing to you and dried up the freedom well. Not to fret. We are on the precipice of a travel renaissance, and I refuse to leap into enlightenment alone.

I'm passing on my travel enthusiasm, knowledge, and narratives in hopes of showing you the rich variety of experiences available to you and convincing you of travel's transformative power.

The book in your hands is the gift I've always wanted to give. My greatest wish is that I can keep one reader from succumbing to fear, guide one seeker down the path of experiential education, or give one person who feels trapped the key to unlock their cuffs.

Sound Familiar?

You wish you traveled more, but there are too many obstacles in the way. You're inspired to pursue a new adventure but don't.

You want to *be* there, but you don't want to *get* there. Sadly, you can't teleport.

Your funds are limited. Your job grants you only a few weeks of vacation time every year. How could you possibly guarantee a favorable return on your travel investment?

The stress of just thinking about planning a bucket-list trip—let alone actually planning it—is dizzying. You don't even have a real bucket list, just an amorphous collection of unfulfilled dreams, "hot" destinations, trendy beaches and hotels.

It's going to take forever to figure it all out, and there are so many options to sift through and compare—who has the time? It would be so much easier to stay home.

Factor in the unhealed scar of your previous travel disaster story (everybody's got one), and it becomes even harder to justify the expenditure. Booking tickets, packing, navigating airports, flying with Rona residue on every seat—why bother?

The entire travel industry seems to be conspiring to trick you into spending more, trap you in binding agreements, penalize you for breaking them, and herd you like cattle toward a tour, town, terminal, seat, station, or situation you never wanted anything to do with.

And then your tectonic plates start to shift. The seed of inspiration awakens a fluttering desire inside of you. In your mind, the place becomes a panacea to all of your woes.

You dive into light research. Perhaps you get serious and buy a guidebook. You browse geotags on Instagram, saving lists of the best restaurants, activities, and photo spots. More inspiration! Right on cue, doubt and anxiety enter stage left. How will you get there? How will you afford it? Who will you go with? How will you tell your boss? Coronavirus!

Pushing through the overwhelm, you search for flights, trying to gauge the financial burden. Are you looking in the wrong place? Are you missing out on better deals? Do the dates you're searching for even work for you? Is this feasible?

You buy the cheapest tickets you can. Flying from NYC to Madrid, you just signed up for an eight-hour layover in Istanbul to save fifty bucks.

As you attempt to plan your dream trip, delusions of grandeur cloud your vision. You throw practical considerations to the curb. You have no method, only a madness to escape. Instead of figuring out where you'll sleep on the third night of your trip, you book a camel ride.

Hurried and incomplete planning poisons your trip. After three brutal flights, you skid into your destination, filthy, hungry, and tired. Factor in the jet lag, and it will take four days for you to feel like yourself again. By then, your trip will be halfway over.

Unanticipated costs and delays mount.

You want a new scarf but buy a Buddha statue. You think it will validate your budding mindfulness practice. It doubles the weight of your daypack. No worries. You're learning how to relinquish attachment. That's what travel is about.

Now utterly unattached to the outcome of your trip, you discard all discipline and rationality. Apathy and recklessness reign. On your last night, toasting to the good life, you stay out late to "live it up." Your nine-hour flight home (the first of three) gives you about as much legroom as the back seat of a coupe. Norwegian Air is serving pasty roly-polies in a tin tray. They claim it's gnocchi. Water? That'll be six dollars.

You don't take the trip; the trip takes you. You pay the price in disappointment and a sad confession: the reality of the place didn't live up to the picture you had of it. It wasn't *your* fault, though.

At least you have some photos to prove you were there. They're blurry and crooked, but you have a new profile pic in there somewhere.

When your friends ask you, "How was your trip?" you recite your polite but convenient lie, "Good!"

Scarred by the disaster of the whole debacle and embarrassed by your own folly, you don't travel again for years.

Congratulations, you will never take one of *those* trips again.

The Premise

In partnership with the US Travel Association, the *Harvard Business Review* surveyed 5,461 adult Americans working more than thirty-five hours per week to demystify what makes a successful travel experience.

The study concluded that "one of the key predictors of vacation ROI is the amount of stress caused by not planning ahead."

There will always be elements of traveling that cannot be predicted. But the real disasters are the preventable ones—missed connections due to faulty planning, underestimations of how long the ride will take, overestimations of what's included in the tour package, terrible sequencing of events, and utter lack of purpose.

Travel planning is like financial planning, but the primary goal is maximizing your time, not your money. With expert planning, you can maximize both.

You can travel with confidence and ease. You don't have to fly by the seat of your pants. You just need to learn how to do it— what to hunt for, what to watch for, and how to reap the dividends of the time, money, and energy you invest.

A well-planned trip will never go out of style. It integrates into, rather than interrupts, your life.

The destination and details may change year to year, but you'll always have to make the same fundamental decisions:

- Where are you going? Why are you going? Who are you going with?
- When's the trip? What's the budget? How will you get there?
- How will you get around once you're there? Where will you eat and sleep?
- Why will the trip be unforgettable?

It sounds simple enough at this macro level. It's when hundreds of microscopic decisions start stacking up that would-be travelers become discouraged and quit.

Not on my watch.

The Promise

This book will simplify the travel process and reframe trip planning as a pleasurable enterprise with enormous, everlasting rewards.

You will learn how to answer the hardest but most crucial question: *Why* do you want to travel? Only after you have identified your trip's purpose will you begin to plan it.

You'll learn how to design an airtight itinerary that safeguards your travel investment and precludes post-trip regret. You'll extract at least as much joy in designing it as you do in taking it.

You'll learn that a little extra effort goes a long way. You'll focus your energy, minimize your expenditures, and maximize your time.

Choosing a travel destination will never again feel like a crapshoot. Your decision on where to travel will be deliberate, reflecting your goals and values. You'll learn how to pick places most likely to fulfill your vision and companions most likely to enhance the journey to your mutual benefit. Trekking in the Scottish Highlands? Cherry blossoms in Japan? Australian coastal road trip? The choices are yours entirely and making them will empower you.

Booking flights will no longer be a fear-laden procedure. You'll learn how, where, and when to confidently and efficiently book flights you're excited to take. You'll learn how to avoid getting duped by fine print or scammy policies. If anything comes up— like a pandemic—your trip will be protected. And so will your peace of mind.

Prepare to become a master in the art of itinerary design. You'll learn to see into the future, considering the flow and arc of your getaway, and build your dream trip as if you were building your dream home.

We're going to kick that pre-trip anxiety, too, by equipping you with the tools, checklists, and mindset to embark with a clear conscience and ensure a seamless return. Plants watered, notifications set, ducks in a row. Row 1, to be exact. (Your ducks fly first class.)

You'll learn how to avoid getting swallowed up in the bowels of the airport and banished to a broken seat in the last row of the plane. Glide through security, relax in a lounge, and be a COVID-resistant beacon of immunity.

When you land, you'll know all your first moves. You'll learn how to acclimatize quickly and ensure you have access to Wi-Fi when you want it. That janky electronics kiosk that sells SIM cards will have to find a different customer.

I'm going to teach you to travel in an exploratory flow state, soaking up all the wonders you set out in search of and more. With an optimized but never overly rigid plan to fall back on, spontaneity and fun will flourish.

You'll move freely and authentically through your destination, mastering the art of mindful travel. Your days as an unsuspecting tourist are numbered.

Documenting your trip will cease to feel like a chore. Instead, everything you create on the road or bring home, from photos to souvenirs, will uplift you for years to come, prolonging the memories you earned.

And your trip won't come to a crashing halt when you dump a week's worth of mail on the kitchen counter. You'll learn how to talk about and, better yet, embody the transformative aspects of your getaway, basking in its afterglow, reenergized and regret-free. When your "normal" life resumes, instead of feeling depleted, you'll feel invigorated.

Above all, you'll come to see that any travel experience, no matter how exotic or far-fetched it may seem, can be yours, that you deserve it, and that it's possible. With confidence, ease, and intention, you'll unlock the unparalleled joy of time amplified, experience savored, and freedom reclaimed.

Rare Form

There's a how-to book for every style of travel. Budget travel. Adventure travel. Long-term travel. Working from anywhere while you travel. Traveling with kids. Traveling in a van. Female solo travel. The list goes on.

And there's a common theme running through them all: sacrifice. Quit your job! Sell your possessions! Skip town, and don't look back!

Sadly, the pervading sentiment about travel is that it is antithetical to "normal" life. Either you suffer through your menial, routine existence as another cog in the workforce, or you escape society's death grip with a one-way ticket to Thailand.

This either-or mentality is inherently flawed. It forces people to choose between their travel dreams and their professional aspirations. It treats normal life as a sickness for which travel is the only remedy.

Instead of writing about one *style* of travel, I'm writing about one *type* of trip, designed for the enormous pool of upwardly mobile young (or young-at-heart) professionals who have the means, desire, and motivation to travel but don't know how to weave a trip into their existing framework of responsibilities.

Many of the tips discussed in this book will help make travel more affordable. But *Get Away!* is not a budget travel manual.

Many of the tips discussed in this book will apply to families. But this book is not a family travel manual. (Also, I don't have kids and can't claim to have any expertise on the matter.)

Many of the tips discussed in this book cite specific locations as examples. But this book is not a guidebook. The advice in this book is not destination-specific; it's destination agnostic.

Books about specific travel styles do overlap with this one, usually in their early chapters, which, like the next chapter, deal with various fears keeping people from taking action. The primary blockade that these books address, which I will also address, is money. The emphasis is on affordability, deal hunting, buying a backpack, eking a few more miles out of the tank. In this book, I acknowledge that expenses matter, but the primary barrier of entry is not money. It's *time*.

This book is at once an ideology, a collection of entertaining and edifying vignettes, and a step-by-step instruction manual for building and taking your ideal trip. After reading *Get Away!* you will feel comfortable and confident designing the kind of travel experience you'll remember forever.

PART 1

PLANNING AND PREPARATION

CHAPTER 1

No More Excuses

"The curtain of habits, the comfortable loom
of words and gestures in which the heart
drowses, slowly rises."
—ALBERT CAMUS

ACCORDING TO HOSTELWORLD's Global Traveler Report, the average American has visited just three nations, and 29 percent of American adults have never been abroad.

The average resident of the United Kingdom has visited ten nations. Obviously, geography plays a role. Crossing the ocean is a much more significant barriers to entry than a train ride or short flight.

But Americans face greater ideological barriers, too. Certain stigmas and attitudes that treat travel as frivolous, irresponsible, or downright impossible have seeped into our cultural zeitgeist.

It is essential to challenge the validity of these attitudes and reexamine the excuses you make for not getting away.

It's Too Much Work

No one ever invokes the "it's too much work" excuse about something they deeply care about.

If you have an unshakable dream or vision for your life—if you're one of the lucky few who is completely locked into your life's purpose—you would never say, "It's too much work." When you want it badly enough, no amount of work is too much.

To say "It's too much work" in the context of travel means there's a disconnect between the perceived work required to execute your vision and the perceived reward. With travel, most people overestimate the work and underestimate the reward.

Think of a getaway as an investment in your ongoing well-being. You exercise today so that you can live a long and healthy life. You save money in your 401(k) so you can comfortably retire. And you stockpile priceless memories that you can summon as a source of happiness anytime in the future—when you're bored, sad, lonely, or maybe when everything's perfect and you just need a good story to tell.

The person who invokes the "too much work" excuse is not wrong to assume that planning their dream will take a lot of work. But mistaking "a lot" for "too much" reflects a lack of self-trust. After all, *you're* the designer. You have the power to create a trip whose value transcends the effort required to obtain it.

I Don't Have Time

No matter the context in which this excuse is uttered, it can be roughly translated to "This isn't important enough to me to prioritize right now." People make time for what really matters to them.

The question is not "How do I free up more time?" It's "How can I make travel a bigger priority?"

If your best friend is getting married, you make time.

If your parent is sick, you make time.

If you land an interview for your dream job, you make time.

You make time for your friends, loved ones, and boss. It's time to make time for yourself. I know you can because you have already started to, by choosing to read this book.

If you break down the trip planning process into smaller steps and put those steps in order, you can accomplish far more than you initially presumed was possible. Simply begin. Beginning will give you clarity, and clarity will propel you forward.

Travel expands time. That's what psychologist William James argued in 1890. According to James, "In youth we may have an absolutely new experience, subjective or objective, every hour of the day. Apprehension is vivid, retentiveness strong, and our recollections of that time, like those of a time spent in rapid and interesting travel, are of something intricate, multitudinous, and long-drawn-out."

Joshua Foer summarizes this concept in *Moonwalking with Einstein: The Art and Science of Remembering Everything*: "Monotony collapses time; novelty unfolds it." In adulthood, routine flattens our recollections into what James calls contentless units. Children live in a constant state of rapture and discovery. Travel restores this childlike wonder and stretches time in our minds. It's not uncommon for travelers to return from an adventure and feel as though they've lived an entire life in a week.

Think about your perception of time in 2020. The headlines, drama, and shock value the year served up with such turbulent regularity made it feel never-ending. Yet the weeks spent in lockdown flew by.

If you've had enough of politics and pandemics, disrupt the tedium of everyday life with travel. The novelty of an immersive trip will amplify your sense of wonder, lengthen your days, and make you a kid again.

Instead of focusing on why you can't travel, focus on why you can't *not* travel. Focus on why you *must* travel. Once you know, you'll have plenty of time.

I Had a Bad Experience

In the heist movie *The Italian Job*, Mos Def's character refuses to break into a home with a large dog on the premises. "I don't do dogs," he says. "I had a bad experience."

"What happened?" his partner asks.

"I HAD a BAD experience."

Everyone has a travel horror story.

You plan a romantic Parisian holiday with your partner. When you arrive in Paris, your suitcase never comes off the carousel. You spend the entire trip on hold with Charles de Gaulle airport, desperately trying to track it down but can't. The lost bag stresses you out, which stresses your partner out, which spoils the romance. You scream at each other over a baguette on a balcony.

Your partner finally gets their bag back (the handle that the luggage tag was attached to broke, and the tag fell off). Problem is, the trip ended two weeks ago and now you're in Minnesota. You refuse to check a bag for the next decade, boycott France, and you and your partner break up.

Boycott *France*? Quit holding grudges against places. They have no secret motives to sabotage your vacation. Be honest. Why did you get stranded in Koh Samet? Was it because the taxi boat driver had it out for you? Or did you forget to check the schedule and oversleep? That's what I thought.

Don't mistake one isolated incident for a trend. No matter how carefully you plan, travel is wrought with uncertainty. That's part of the fun. Next time, cover your tracks. Temper the risks and randomness of traveling—the spider bite on your eyelid in Costa Rica that caused your whole face to swell, the theft of your shoes when you customarily left them outside a guesthouse in Laos, the hotel in San Sebastian that regrets to inform you they have no record of your reservation.

You and I could have exactly the same trip planned but take two completely different trips. On the first day of your trip, you could be sipping a Negroni at the hotel bar and find yourself sitting next to Matthew McConaughey. Meanwhile, just outside of the same hotel, I could fall into a manhole and sprain my tibia. You never know.

If getting out of your comfort zone matters to you whatsoever, start by embracing the discomfort of things potentially going wrong. Assume they might, but don't expect they will. Give your next trip a fair chance to blow your mind. And make sure the handle of your suitcase doesn't rip off on the way to Antibes.

It's Too Expensive

By far, the most common question I receive about my travels is, "How do you afford it?"

You won't hear me tell you to sell your nightstand on Craigslist to be able to afford seventeen more ramen dinners in Vietnam. But travel does not have to be expensive. Here are some ways to minimize the financial burden:

- Choose a cheaper destination. Try Montenegro instead of Croatia, or Cambodia instead of Japan.
- Travel in the off-season or shoulder season. Rates skyrocket during peak season.
- Plan better! Planning gives you time to read the fine print, catch hidden fees, and avoid baloney policies. Plus, you won't make as many costly decisions out of desperation.
- Use points and miles whenever possible. For most people, flights are the biggest trip expense. Some extra effort here can go a long way.
- Stop buying dumb stuff that you don't actually need. Tighten your spending habits and save. To stack extra cash for trips, I've forgone alcohol, TV, Postmates, and I'm in the arduous process of kicking my shoe habit. It adds up.

Your trip can be as lavish or economical as you want it to be. "Expensive" is all relative anyway. Your "balling out" could be someone else's "slumming it." Your "roughing it" could be someone else's honeymoon.

I'm Scared for My Health and Safety

Leisure travel, even if permitted, felt irresponsible in 2020. All travel-thwarting virus concerns were valid, and I shared those concerns.

But if you're scared for your health, don't avoid traveling; avoid *not* traveling.

Psychologist Jessica de Bloom studied the effect of vacations on health and well-being. After tracking travelers' physical and emotional well-being before, during, and after various types of vacations, de Bloom reported increases in joy and contentment due to the replenishment of depleted cognitive resources. News-flash: occasionally distancing yourself from routine hassles makes you feel better!

One set of de Bloom's data came from travelers who had taken nine-day active winter sports vacations, although her hypothesis held up among travelers who took short vacations in the Netherlands and longer summer vacations. The health benefits of vacations, she found, were not defined by the type of trip travelers took as much as the degree to which they were able to savor their experience.

The mental health benefits of travel are widely documented. The Wisconsin Rural Women's Health Study took a random sample of women in Wisconsin and measured their odds of depression over a six-year span. The odds of depression increased in women who took vacations only once every two years compared to women who took vacations twice or more per year. The study even found that a decrease in the frequency of vacations correlated to a decrease in marital satisfaction. Travel saves cheese-head marriages, and it could save yours, too.

Expedia reported that 91 percent of travelers set out, in part, to eliminate stress and anxiety. It's paradoxical that health concerns about traveling induce so much stress. Most people's health fears are tragically myopic; they fail to take into account the myriad long-term, vitality-enhancing benefits of travel, such as resilience, motivation, and perspective.

Travel remaps your brain by increasing its neuroplasticity. Predictability and routine lead to cognitive decay, but new environments, challenges, and sensations shock your synapses and take your brain off autopilot. Clinical neuropsychologist Dr. Paul Nussbaum affirms, "Travel is an important behavior that promotes brain health and builds resilience." Solving problems, deciphering languages, experimenting, and exposing yourself to new experiences sprouts so many dendrites in your brain that "it literally begins to look like a jungle."

What kind of brain do you want? A crusty spaghetti cerebellum clumped in a colander, or a flowering forest of blazing neurons?

Travel reduces stress and keeps your brain sharp, but the benefits don't stop there. Travel even improves your personality. A 2013 study published in the *Journal of Personality and Social Psychology* tracked the personality development of "sojourners." The study confirmed a benefit of travel that most travelers feel is true but perhaps have never had a way to validate; traveling is associated with increases in openness and agreeableness as well as a decrease in neuroticism.

I'm slightly skeptical about that last point because I've traveled quite a bit, yet still gnaw my cuticles and have saved this document four times while writing this paragraph. Nonetheless, the study's findings suggest that conscientious, international sojourners become better versions of themselves by spending time abroad.

Many Americans dream of traveling in retirement, but you might want to hit the road sooner to ensure you live that long. A comprehensive survey conducted by the Global Coalition on Aging determined that frequent vacations are an essential component of a healthy path to old age. The survey found that men who did not take an annual vacation had a 20 percent higher risk of death and 30 percent higher risk of death from heart disease. Women who vacationed every six years or less had a significantly higher risk of developing heart disease than women who vacationed at least twice per year.

So if travel is proven to be beneficial for your emotional, mental, and physical wellness, what's left to fear?

What about the driving in Sri Lanka? It's utter pandemonium! No lanes, no seat belts, unpaved roads!

What about the air quality in Shanghai? It's like smoking two packs a day!

Also: COVID! I'm out!

Indeed, unforeseen threats do exist abroad (we'll touch on this more in Chapter 13). But they also exist at home. Don't let your irrational fears keep you from tapping into travel's boundless wellspring of vitality.

Consider, last, what would happen to a society whose members all valued vacations more highly and took them more frequently. Swedish environmental psychologist Terry Hartig argues that vacations not only restore depleted individual resources but also our capacity to provide support and companionship to vulnerable members of our communities. Hartig calls this phenomenon collective restoration, an oft-neglected benefit of an entire population placing greater emphasis on travel. And it makes perfect sense. Can we fully show up to support the vulnerable, suffering, or elderly members of our society if we as individuals are not fully restored? No, because as Hartig puts it, "Depletion of individual resources has social consequences."

In 2020, earthlings grappled with unprecedented contagion. But the restorative benefits of travel are viral, too. We must travel not only for our own health and wellness but also for each other's.

I'm Scared It Will Hurt My Career

Americans are terrified of taking breaks from work—even when their employer is paying them to do so.

Paid time off—what a dreamy concept! I'll go to the Bahamas, and you'll keep paying me as if I never left.

But Americans are scared that leaving work will jeopardize their job security. According to a Skift survey, nearly 42 percent of Americans took zero vacation days in 2014.

Americans love the idea of PTO in principle. A 2017 study from Project: Time Off found that 95 percent of survey participants believed it was important to use their vacation days. But the same survey found that 55 percent of those participants left precious PTO unused. A Glassdoor survey found that only 23 percent of workers used all of their PTO.

This phenomenon of work martyrdom saddens me. There is clearly an embedded stigma against not working in American society.

In fact, the stigma is rooted in policy. The United States is the only nation out of thirty-eight members of the Organisation for Economic Co-operation and Development (OECD) that does not mandate paid vacation days. (In contrast, the United Kingdom mandates twenty-eight days, and every other European OECD nation mandates at least twenty days.)

Career-related travel fears are so real for American workers that, according to Glassdoor, two in three Americans report working while on vacation.

Even when Americans get away, they're not fully gone. Due to the ease of connectivity, work follows them. Addicted to busyness and devices, people feel defined by their performance at work and terrified of falling behind. They worry that while they're gone, their employers will deem them dispensable. What if the company makes cutbacks? Who will be first on the chopping block? Showing up to work even (and especially) when it's not required shows dedication. Forgoing vacation is seen as a form of self-preservation.

Ironically, an Expedia Vacation Deprivation study determined that "the pressure to be available may be self-imposed—only a small number of respondents say their managers (17 percent), junior staff (10 percent), and clients (12 percent) expect them to check in daily while on vacation, proving most people need to simply give themselves permission to unplug."

Perhaps the most paralyzing of all job-related travel deterrents is the fear of returning from vacation to a mountain of accumulated work. (In Chapter 9, we'll discuss essential planning procedures to ensure a seamless reentry into both your home and office.)

Ambitious workers may argue that their unused PTO is less about not falling behind and more about trying to get ahead. These high achievers may be surprised to learn that according to a *Harvard Business Review* study, workers who took more than eleven vacation days were 30 percent more likely to receive a raise. When total vacation days taken dropped below ten, the likelihood of receiving a raise or bonus dropped from 65.4 percent to 34.6 percent.

The only reasonable justification for these statistics is that vacations boost employee productivity and performance.

Sure enough, research overwhelmingly shows that time away from the office leads to increased motivation, creativity, innovation, happiness, and morale. Travel helps workers avoid burnout and recharge.

In 2007, *Businessweek* reported that vacation deprivation results in increased mistakes and resentment toward coworkers. Who wouldn't snap at Jenny in HR when they postpone their trip to Cinque Terre for the twelfth straight summer?

A particularly intriguing 2014 study from the *Academy of Management Journal*, coauthored by social psychologist and Columbia Business School professor Adam Galinsky, tracked the innovations of top fashion designers across eleven years of collections based on the executives' foreign work experience. The study found that creative directors with immersive international experience produced collections that external audiences deemed more novel and useful. Although this study focuses on professional experiences abroad specifically in the fashion industry, it suggests a strong correlation between foreign experience and creative innovation.

Do your coworkers, clients, boss, organization, and yourself a favor: take a vacation, and make it count.

I'm Scared of the Unknown

Fear of the unknown is a healthy expression of our innate self-protecting instincts. It becomes dangerous when it causes us to misjudge risk and holds us back from exploring new domains. Inaction is a much greater threat than uncertainty.

The hazards we imagine we'll have to confront when we venture into the unknown are always scarier in our imagination than they are in reality. What we gain when we face our fears makes beating them fruitful.

Albert Camus hit it on the head in 1937:

What gives value to travel is fear. It breaks down a kind of inner structure we have. One can no longer cheat—hide behind the hours spent at the office or at the plant (those hours we protest so loudly, which protect us so well from the pain of being alone). Travel robs us of such refuge. Far from our own people, our own language, stripped of all our props, deprived of our masks (one doesn't know the fare on the streetcars, or anything else), we are completely on the surface of ourselves. But also, soul-sick, we restore to every being and every object its miraculous value.

Are you cheating? Are you hiding? Embrace the unknown. Book a trip. Lift the curtain of comfort you live behind.

But I Love My Normal Life

I have a few friends who don't travel. They simply aren't interested. They have the means to take a trip, but they don't feel the need.

"I love my life here in California," one says. "I'm obsessed with my work. If I traveled, I'd have to leave all of that behind."

To which I respond, "Would you, though?"

I love that you love your normal life. I would never ask you to relinquish it. But there's no reason travel can't be a part of it. What if travel made you love your normal life even more? A dose of the unfamiliar usually does the trick.

University of California sociologists Cathy Stein Greenblat and John H. Gagnon explore the idea of travel as a voluntary, albeit temporary, move from the realm of the familiar into the world of strangers. They argue that leisure experiences provide "an experience of conquering new worlds, of having a sense of personal efficacy and accomplishment."

People who love their normal lives are present to their circumstances. Travel shows you that your ability to feel good isn't dependent on the formula you've created at home. You can feel content no matter where you are.

You're Excused

The adage is true in travel, too. Absence really does make the heart grow fonder.

To fully appreciate what you have, you have to distance yourself from it occasionally. Not abandon it, just view it from afar, and then up close again, anew.

Everything you fear about travel is what makes it so valuable. The real trip is not from one time zone into another. It's straight into the fear that's holding you back. In it, you'll find everything you desire: personal development, professional advancement, good health, fullness, balance, and joy.

You have just as much time as anyone else and the same finite life.

Perhaps you tried to get away before, and you're reeling from the time, money, and energy you think you wasted. You can bounce back and do it right this time.

Perhaps you didn't grow up traveling and don't think of yourself as a traveler. You can declare a new reality and become one now.

If finances scare you, remember, you're allowed to set the budget and decide how lavish (or not) you want your trip to be.

You are in control. You have the tools and ability to design a trip according to your precise specifications.

The stakes are too high to travel through a screen for the rest of your life. No matter how many elephants there are in the parade, you can't feel the ground rumble on a virtual safari.

Travel helps you clarify your preferences and priorities. If they're already clear, it sharpens them.

Not yet convinced that the risk is worth the reward? Don't know how to pull it off? I'll walk you through it step by step. First, you'll need to get your mind right.

CHAPTER 2

Mindful Travel Mastery

"Travel is fatal to prejudice, bigotry, and narrow-
mindedness, and many of our people need it sorely on
these accounts. Broad, wholesome, charitable views
of men and things cannot be acquired by vegetating
in one little corner of the earth all one's lifetime."

—MARK TWAIN

MOST TRAVELERS ARE mindless, not mindful.

Mindless travelers are pillagers of places. They storm in, get their angles just right, snap their pics, and leave. They try on cultures like outfits to buy and wear once, without taking the tags off, only to return later for a full refund. They want new experiences but only if those experiences require neither effort nor further education.

Mindful travelers give more than they take. They move through the world as ambassadors rather than pirates. They reflect on why they're going instead of obsessing about where they're going. They prepare and educate themselves about their destination's culture and customs and make intentional choices about how to interact with local people and inhabit foreign spaces.

The psychology of leisure discussed in the previous chapter referred primarily to "vacations." Although vacations can certainly be mindful enterprises, I prefer the connotations of "trips." Trips are riskier in the sense that comfort is not their primary aim, but their transformative upside is greater. Unlike vacations devoted solely to R&R, trips aim for deeper cultural immersion and produce memories that never expire—memories worth far more than the resources expended to attain them.

Maybe someday traveling will regress to a purer version of itself, where being at a destination will become more important than having been there. Maybe someday life will. Maybe that day is today.

The Joy of Anticipation

When does a trip start? When you begin packing? When your Uber pulls up? When you land at your destination? I would argue that your trip begins the moment you start planning it.

Although people tend to think about trips as simply the "being there" part, trip planning is no less a part of your trip than life planning is a part of your life.

Planning is supposed to be fun and it is, because anticipating a pleasurable experience is, in itself, pleasurable. A UK study comparing the subjective well-being of vacationers and non-vacationers concluded that those waiting to go on a holiday felt happier about their family, economic situation, and health than those without an upcoming holiday in the calendar.

These days, everyone wants instant gratification. But instantly gratifying experiences don't feel as good as ones we've worked and waited for. Think about how you feel when you order something you love online, but the package take a few weeks to arrive. Every day, you check the tracking number. You're exhilarated every time someone knocks on your door. Each false alarm hurts more than the one before it, yet your eagerness builds. When the package finally arrives, it feels even better to finally open it.

When you have a trip planned and booked in advance, with a bespoke itinerary and every detail accounted for, your investment starts paying dividends instantly. Every day leading up to your departure is laden with the joy of anticipation, the excitement of knowing you have a package in the mail on its way to you right now, getting closer every day. The box is huge, has "Fragile, Handle with Care" stickers on it, and requires a signature.

It's easy to dish out perfect scores when we evaluate future events. When we can tell ourselves anything about how an event will transpire, we tend to tell ourselves what makes us happiest. This phenomenon has a name: rosy prospection. It's the reason that, when done right, planning a trip can be one of the most enjoyable parts of it.

After all, there's always a chance that the event you're awaiting might not happen. Who knows, some freakish contagion could rip across the globe, kill over four million people, and make it socially acceptable to wear sweatpants at the office. But an even more formidable nemesis claims the title of Chief Vacation Ruiner: expectations.

I can't knock anyone for looking at life through rose-colored glasses. If people started knocking me for that, I'd get knocked out. Besides, it's just as normal to give biased evaluations of future experiences as it is of past experiences. We tell whatever story we need to tell to validate our dreams and justify our failures.

In later chapters, I'll talk more about how to savor your getaway as it unfolds. Here's a teaser: if you thought looking forward to an event was gratifying, wait until you put on your foggy rose-tinted memory goggles. Looking forward to remembering your trip when it's over might save the whole enchilada from becoming a giant nothing-burger.

Even if the fragile package you've been anxiously awaiting contains two pairs of shoes a size apart, the smaller of which turns out to be too small and the larger, too big, you'll have a new pleasurable outcome to await: your refund when you send back both pairs. Return shipping might not be included, and you really needed those espadrilles, but the joy is yours to keep.

Skin in the Game

The inclination to relinquish responsibility for planning your own trip presumes that planning is necessarily a hassle. But beyond the evidence that planning is, in itself, an enjoyable experience, another glaring fact about planning begs not to be overlooked: it increases the odds of the trip occurring.

The more skin in the game you have, the greater sense of control you have, and the more determined you become to reap the hedonic payout of your investment.

Excuse me, did you say payout? Traveling will make me rich?

Yes. Rich in perspective, awareness, and appreciation.

A psychology professor at North Carolina State University pinpointed an additional benefit of planning your own travel experience: "proactive coping." All stress stems from a perceived lack of control or uncertainty about the future, but gathering information—for example, about how to get from Houston to Antwerp in no more than two flights with the shortest possible layover—and accumulating resources like approved vacation days or money, dissolves stress. Proactive coping is about goal management more than risk management. By being proactive, travelers can ward off stressors, thoughtfully allocate their funds and energy, and commit to conquering challenges. It's empowering.

Many people don't want to plan their own trips because they don't trust themselves to avoid disasters. With all the uncertainty that travel brings, is that even possible? No amount of planning can completely rule out theft, loss, or volcano eruptions.

The goal is not total immunity from bad luck or lousy circumstances. If the cards don't fall in your favor, that's one thing. But when you take full responsibility, you can more easily forgive yourself when fate intervenes, knowing you did your best to prevent calamities.

Another common objection to trip planning is that no amount of planning ever seems like enough. It's like creating a work of abstract art. How do you know when it's done? My rule is, if it's possible to make a reservation for any service or activity, I do. I allocate my leisure time so that I don't waste my entire trip figuring out what to do, eat, and see. I plan in order to earn the freedom to deviate from my plan without suffering.

Many married people consider their wedding days to be perfect days. It's not surprising; that single day took months of preparation. Every detail was accounted for, customized for maximum beauty and emotional impact.

Planning a trip is like planning a wedding—but better. You don't have to worry about making everyone else happy. The impetus for every decision is to maximize your own happiness, aiming for perfection on your own terms.

As is true for weddings, you can't guarantee that everything will transpire according to plan. There will be hiccups. Still, you can strive for your ideal version. Plan your trip with the same care and diligence with which you would plan your wedding, and magic will ensue.

Do the Honors

Most people treat time as limitless and money as scarce. I have the privilege of believing the opposite is true: money is limitless and time is scarce.

Regardless of how you feel about money, your vacation time is undeniably scarce. That's the beauty of it.

It's a contract with yourself. You carve out the time—a duration neither piddly nor unreasonably long—and you invest your care and attention into maximizing that time. You honor every minute of your trip through the effort you put into planning it and the quality of your awareness while you're living it. You trust that the quality of your days and the quality of your planning will be proportional.

If the only way your trip transforms you is by causing you to honor "ordinary" time (your everyday, non-exotic, non-bucket-list time) with the same zest you honor travel time, that's a win.

There's enough uncertainty in the world to expose the futility of the most intricate plan. Therefore, the goal of your getaway should be optimization, not control.

Travel is fun because it's surprising. Revel in that element of surprise, but also prepare for it so you don't waste your time.

You can follow all the advice in this book, but I promise, you will not have a perfect trip. The most perfect thing that could happen to you is by traveling, you became a more mindful individual, someone who honors time through the dance of travel.

At Your Leisure

"It's quite a wonderful thing," E. M. Forster once said, "the possession of leisure." But what is leisure? Most Americans tend to think of it as the opposite of work—a state of non-activity.

This conception of leisure is misguided. Thinking of leisure as an escape from work and a means to an end makes it impossible to possess and enjoy it fully.

Leisure *is* work, just a different kind of work. It's the work of wonder and contemplation.

German philosopher Josef Pieper described it as "the restoration of man's inner eye...the point at which the three elements of leisure come to a focus: relaxation, effortlessness, and superiority of 'active leisure' to all functions."

Relaxation alone is not enough. Lazing on the beach all day is not enough. We're talking about the total rejuvenation of the spirit by means of essential and sometimes uncomfortable contemplation. We're talking about inner harmony.

According to Pieper, "Leisure is only possible when we are at one with ourselves. We tend to overwork as a means of self-escape, as a way of trying to justify our existence."

Do the work of not working. Learn to be at peace with yourself. Treat leisure as a necessity rather than an optional indulgence.

Rich in Experience

Cornell psychologist Thomas Gilovich is an expert on hedonic relativism, which compares the happiness produced by different types of investments. His recent experiments have proven what many of us eventually realize or have always suspected: experiences yield greater happiness than material possessions.

What makes experiences such excellent investments? What makes material purchases inferior?

It's a matter of durability. Material purchases feel good at the moment you make them. After that initial dopamine wave crashes, the lasting value of material possessions comes from their physical durability. The highest quality goods are the ones that last the longest. Your new sofa will last twenty years, but your trip to South Africa will be over in February.

Trips offer a different kind of durability—psychological durability. Memories of experiences don't deflate and fade like saggy sofa cushions. They grow ever sweeter in our minds.

According to Gilovich, "Although material purchases do indeed last longer, it is notable that when asked to make retrospective evaluations, people tend to say that what they paid for their experiential purchases represented money better spent than what they paid for their material purchases."

When you buy an experience, you gain a story. The value of stories is incomparable and everlasting. When people first consider a new travel experience, they rarely consider the endless sustenance the memory of their adventure will provide. They tend to think about the experience as an item of clothing they can only hope will never fray and still be in style thirty years from now.

Experiences never depreciate. The older stories get, the more psychologically beneficial they become. Memory smooths out their kinks, and even the most disastrous trips become giving trees of happy recollections or fruitful lessons.

Gilovich explains, "It is easier to identify deeper meaning and compulsory benefits in painful experiences than in possessions that did not live up to expectations."

The advantages of experiential purchases do not end there. In our competitive society, comparisons can easily lower self-esteem.

The best part about experiential purchases such as travel, unlike material purchases, is that "they are less likely to spark potentially deflating social comparisons."

The value of experiences is so subjective that I hesitate to recommend specific destinations. There's a beach called Balos on the northwest tip of Crete's Gramvousa Peninsula. It's a pinkish tombolo accessible via a cliffside road. Barely wide enough for two cars to pass, with a stone wall on one side and sheer drop-off on the other, the road is almost as memorable as the beach itself. Arriving at the parking lot, hiking down to the umbrella-lined sandbar, and flinging myself into the Aegean is one of my favorite memories from four seasons in Greece.

Naturally, when my uncle told me he was planning to visit Crete and asked for advice, I told him Balos was not to be missed. Three months later, when I asked him how his trip was, he described his miserable excursion to the beach. He had taken a boat there from Chania instead of driving (why didn't I think of that?), but the Greek *meltemi*, the dreaded northerly wind, got the best of his vessel. He arrived nauseous at a cloudy Balos, the lowlight of his trip, and won't be asking me for travel recommendations anytime soon.

On the other hand, if I love my Peloton and my uncle is looking for an interactive fitness bike and asks me for a recommendation, I won't hesitate to recommend it because I know his Peloton will be exactly the same as mine.

Material possessions have objective values, but experiences have subjective values. That's the best thing about them.

Performance Art

Travel has completely changed for me in the last decade. It used to be about searching. Now it's about sharing.

Just as I started to become more aware of the difference between these two modes of travel, I came across a piece of writing that greatly influenced my philosophy on travel. It's a 1989 journal article published by Judith Adler at the University of Chicago called "Travel as Performed Art."

Adler's argument is that travel is a creative, self-generative act. In travel, as in any other kind of art, there are styles. What kind of artist you are is based on the extent to which you adhere to or deviate from existing styles. The artistic traveler is conscious of all the preestablished "ways" and synthesizes them into her or his own distinct performance.

According to Adler, travel functions as a work of art when it is "undertaken and executed with a primary concern for the meanings discovered, created, and communicated."

Exploring what a trip *means* is different than merely taking it. Mining for meaning requires awareness of one's self and one's destination. It requires deliberate, moment-to-moment attention.

To describe travel as performed art suggests that there is an audience watching the performance. That audience is not your Instagram followers. It's you. That's why the best performances are the most authentic ones.

A flawless travel performance is not staged, fictionalized, or embellished. It's the one most in tune with the traveler's real desires, fears, and goals. It's filling your itinerary with only sights and activities that intuitively speak to you. It's effortless, fun, and loaded with wonder.

What it all comes down to is experiencing a place according to your own curiosity and values, not someone else's. As soon as you try to imitate a precooked agenda rather than cooking up your own raw experience, you've forgotten your lines, so to speak, and spoiled the performance. If you treat travel like art and create it rather than following a script, you'll be amazed at what splendid realities you can conjure.

Break a leg.

A Place in the Sun

Whenever I'm skeptical about the value proposition of a certain activity, wondering if the trail will be too slick or the sunrise too early, I think of a quote from travel writer Paul Theroux: "My only boast in travel is my effort."

A Yellowstone National Park ranger told me that 90 percent of visitors don't venture more than fifteen minutes away from the parking lot. The principle applies to tourists everywhere. People are lazy. Tourists complain about other tourists, make no extra effort to avoid or distinguish themselves from them, then become exactly the kind of tourist they loathe. Only additional effort can break the cycle. It doesn't have to be a lot.

When I visited Dubrovnik in late July, the city was flooded with tourists, the midday heat was unbearable, and it was not a charming scene. The next morning, I woke up early to wander through a vacant old town at dawn. It was enchanting.

If you hate waking up early, find another way to exert an additional 10 percent effort. Plan ahead to prepare a picnic. Turn down a back street instead of eating on the main drag. The action may be off the beaten path.

Still and Still Moving

Mindful travel is considered and immersive.

It means celebrating with locals, rather than watching them celebrate.

It means thanking people in their language, not yours.

It means adapting to the rhythm and pace of a place rather than imposing your rhythm onto it.

If you see a procession of sauntering Greeks taking their sundown stroll known as a *volta*, join them. Be in no hurry to begin or finish.

Find balance between routine and indulgence. Climb stairs in the morning; eat pistachio gelato at night.

Give every place its fair shot. Don't prematurely besmirch anywhere on hearsay. Trust that your destination wants to pleasantly surprise you.

Look for glimmers of shared humanity. The kumquat farmer in Malaysia has a family, too. Don't act like an alien—or treat him like one—just because you've never seen such stubby citrus.

Document scenes with your senses. Heed T. S. Eliot's advice: "Be still and still moving into another intensity." Let your imagination scream while you remain silent.

Take public transportation. Maybe you'll get clotheslined by a turnstile you walk through in the wrong direction. The point is, you tried.

Seek solace in nature. Tap into the spiritual dimension. Embrace episodes of isolation in the mountains, a botanical garden, or simply while sipping your morning macchiato.

Absorb the character of a place at the local market. Buy a bag of cashews and some apricots. Smile at the lady.

Leave the place better than you found it. The question now is, what place?

CHAPTER 3

Destination Discovery

"You take delight not in a city's seven
or seventy wonders, but in the answer
it gives to a question of yours."

—ITALO CALVINO

I REMEMBER STUDYING immigration in US history class and learning about push and pull factors. Push factors, like the Irish potato famine, drive people out of one place, and pull factors draw them into another.

With travel, we're all being pulled in a million different directions. There are, after all, infinite destinations to travel to, each with its own allure. The bucket lists of even the most seasoned travelers always seem to regenerate.

The mystique of a place may inspire you. An exotic image may strike a chord. But for a getaway to truly deliver, before you decide *where* you're going, you must get clear about *why* you're going.

What's pushing you?

On shorter trips, with smaller commitments of time and resources, there's less at stake. Have fun at the wedding in Charleston—what more is there to say?

On longer trips, it's easier to veer off course and lose focus on your real objective. The days roll by like weeks in quarantine. Or the objective is too broad—the same reason that New Year's resolutions hardly ever stick.

Always distinguish between negative and positive push factors. A negative push factor is a fear-based motivation for leaving. It's a way of avoiding conflict or discomfort. Instead of facing the dragon head-on, you run away, making the ultimate travel mistake of thinking your problems won't all be exactly where you left them when you return.

A positive push factor is aspirational. It's an innate desire, a reaching for some higher state of self-awareness. For example, if you notice yourself struggling with feelings of dependency or low self-confidence, perhaps the purpose you declare for your trip would be to discover pockets of solitude that remind you of your innate power. Four months later, you might actualize that declared purpose at a meditation retreat or on a distant dune in the Gobi Desert amid a tribe of Kazakh eagle hunters. You tell me.

Focus on what's pulling you only after you've gotten clear on what's pushing you.

On Purpose

You can spend a lifetime gathering inspiration from social media, travel magazines, and anecdotes from your friends. But at a certain point, you have to let your intuition guide you. You don't want to pick a destination out of unlimited options. You want the destination to pick you because it's the only option. For that to happen, you must look inward.

A getaway is not a postponement of reality. There is no such thing as postponing reality! Reality will follow you deep into the red sands of Wadi Rum, across the Tibetan plateau, and along the coral coast of Queensland.

A getaway is a melodious interlude on the album of your life. It's an opportunity for reflection and a foray into a new frequency of possibility.

What statement do you want to make by taking this particular trip at this particular time? Challenge yourself to look beyond superficial motivations. Let these prompts guide you:

- What I'm excited to learn about myself is…
- Besides seeing beautiful sites, one side benefit I'm hoping this trip will bring about is…
- On the surface, the reason why I want to travel is…But when I think about it more deeply, I realize that it's really about…
- In addition to sightseeing, I intend to use this time to think about…
- I know this trip will test my…I'm also using it to hone my…
- A successful getaway would be one that…
- After this trip, I want to be…

The ideal guiding mantra for a getaway would fit this structure:

My trip will generate [blank] by making time/space for [blank], which will lead to my ultimate transformative goal of [blank].

Write it down. Carry it with you in your wallet. Look at it on the road. Remember the intention you set and recalibrate as necessary.

QUEST BEHAVIOR

Turning your trip into a quest is a surefire way to imbue it with meaning. If you set out with a clear mission, you'll never be confused about your trip's purpose.

Perhaps you're one of a growing number of travelers looking to track down your family lineage. Travel brands are catching on to the heritage travel trend. For example, Airbnb partnered with genetic insight giant 23andMe to offer DNA-based global quests.

Tournaments, festivals, and special events can provide an added layer of purpose to your trip. My friends and I once followed the US National Team at the FIFA World Cup. We did our best to get to all of the United States' matches. If we couldn't, we found the next best match. The sense of accomplishment I felt in scoring front-row tickets (with some luck from the lottery system) to the United States' opening match against Ghana in Natal, and the excitement of being at the epicenter of a global event, spurred me on.

Perhaps you have an ongoing quest or collection of experiences you're building—the world's best golf courses or amusement parks, rare celestial phenomena, or iconic locations from literature or cinema.

Quests unlock destinations you might not otherwise visit. Your exact location becomes less important than achieving the goal you've established.

Kindred Spirits

Mark Twain once said, "I have found out there ain't no surer way to find out whether you like people or hate them than to travel with them." He was right. Travel really is the best way to discover compatibility. But when it comes to choosing a travel companion, we can all agree it's preferable to know how you feel about the other person *before* the trip.

If you want to screen potential BFF contenders, play mini-golf or get bagels. Reserve your getaway for a companion you already know you get along with swimmingly.

But it's not that simple. I get along with all of my friends, but I wouldn't want to take a multiday trip with all of them. How do you choose? Your preferences and purposes should align as much as possible. Beyond those fundamentals, here are some essential questions to help you weed out the wannabes:

- **What kinds of activities do they enjoy, and at what level of intensity do they prefer to enjoy them?** If you love wine tasting and beach lazing, but they want to bungee jump and summit volcanoes, your mutual affinities for ice cream and karaoke won't bridge the gap.
- **Do your dietary preferences align?** Will they be boiling beans in the camping stove they packed while you're making waterfront sushi reservations? If they merely want convenience, but you want Michelin stars, brace for disaster when you try to split the bill at Cheval Blanc in Basel.
- **Speaking of money, do you share similar spending philosophies?** Are you both clear about what level of trip this is? If you're envisioning helicopter flights and yacht charters but your buddy would rather walk an hour than pay for an Uber, the price is not right.
- **At what pace do they operate?** Do they insist on hitting every hidden gem in the guidebook, even if it means

sacrificing depth for distance? Or are they content to sit at the resort sipping piña coladas all day?

- **What's their standard of cleanliness?** Are they a germophobe who pinches the coverlet off every hotel bed and flings it into the corner of the room (because they obviously never wash those things), while you're more of the "yeah, it smells vaguely of diapers in here, and there's an odd stain on this pillowcase, but we're staying for only one night, so it will be fine" type? Red flag.

- **How do they feel about nightlife?** Do they drink or smoke? If I say the word "club," and you start thinking about a nine-iron while your travel companion thinks about DJ sets in Ibiza, it might be time to cork the Patrón.

- **Can you share a room with them?** Sure, it might save you money, but have you ever done it? Do they snore? Do they smell? Do they blast the Rap Caviar playlist on Spotify while they're brushing their teeth at 1:00 a.m., take inappropriately long showers, frequently forget to flush, and turn the thermostat down to sixty-six, mumbling mumbo jumbo about their circadian rhythm?

- **Speaking of circadian rhythms, when do they wake up and go to sleep?** Will they be up at dawn for sunrise walking tours while you're sleeping through breakfast and reading on the balcony in a bathrobe?

- **If you wanted or needed to split up for a short time, would they be cool with that?** If they wanted to, would you? I once went hiking with my friend to an alpine lake. He set off in front of me at a blistering pace. I could not and did not want to keep up. I didn't see him again for two and a half hours. When I met him at the top, he had already jumped in the lake, eaten lunch, and was ready to descend.

He was under the impression that we were hiking together, as in on the same trail. I was under the impression we were hiking *together*. Don't make the same mistake I did.

- **Are they willing to compromise?** If you want to take a cooking class, but they want to take a jungle hike, can you meet in the middle and do something both aromatic *and* dewy? Thai massages?
- **Here's the big one: can you plan together?** How it feels to plan with someone is highly indicative of how it will feel to travel with them. Planning should be easier when you do it with your companion. If, instead, it feels like a school project for which you got paired with the class dodo bird, call an audible because that C– will be your grade, too.

Planning a trip should bring you closer. Let's say you decide to travel with a friend you speak to on the phone once a month. Get ready to start talking to that person multiple times per week. If you're not increasingly more excited to talk to your running mate each time, sound the alarm.

QUITE A COMPLEMENT

It doesn't usually work out well to choose a travel buddy whose interests don't match yours. But if the two of you have complementary skillsets or modes of operating, it might be a travel buddy match made in heaven.

I love to orchestrate itineraries and day-by-day plans. My friend Mike always finds the best bars, restaurants, exhibitions, and events on a given night. So when we went to London for Wimbledon, I secured the tennis tickets and designed a loose schedule for each day. Mike filled in the gaps, scoring us dinner reservations and tickets to pop-up events I might never have discovered on my own. We both contributed where and how it felt most natural and enhanced the collective trip in the process. That's the way it should be.

I'LL BE HONEST

As in any successful relationship, the success of your choice of travel companion comes down to communication.

Sometimes, even with close friends, we avoid or tread carefully around certain topics. Family members may say things that irritate us, and we let those comments slide because we know they mean well. Those people may be closer to us than anyone else in our lives, but in the vacuum that is a vacation, you must feel comfortable sharing your hopes, fears, and anxieties with your travel partner. On a trip designed to enhance your personal liberation, you certainly don't want to feel like you can't be yourself or say what's on your mind at any time.

HEADS-UP

After you choose who you're going to travel with, quality communication remains paramount.

Whenever I'm planning a trip with someone new, I give them a disclaimer about myself that goes something like this:

I eat a lot. Food will be a controlling element of every day for me. At restaurants, I may order two to three times as much food as you. Don't worry, I'll make sure to pay for my fair share. Sometimes I get hangry. If I ever suddenly become irritable and impatient, I apologize in advance. I will do my best to prevent that from happening by always carrying snacks. Sometimes I may need to make detours to buy more snacks. Snacks are very important to me. Oh, and I need breakfast in order to be the best version of myself. Please prepare yourself for these eventualities.

I might even add this booster statement:

> Photography is my MO. I do not intend to put my photography ahead of our mutual well-being and the flow of our trip. However, there may be times when I need to linger a bit longer at certain attractions. I have a few specific sites in mind that I'd like to take my time at. If you ever feel like I'm holding you back, please tell me.

Asking someone to travel with you can be daunting because, when you ask, you have to be prepared for them to say yes! Before they agree, both of you should be totally clear about what you're getting into. Address all elephants in all rooms. Acknowledge your differences and discuss how you'd work around them or use them to your mutual advantage. Communicate candidly about your proposition so no one has to secretly wonder if they made an enormous mistake. If the trip manifests, you'll only feel a tighter bond with your companion when you finally depart.

LEAVE ME ALONE

Solo travel is not my preferred mode. It may be easier to make decisions, but it's more challenging emotionally, especially if you're not accustomed to solitude.

A solo trip is a high-risk, high-reward play. Even the loneliest solo trip will boost your resilience. Who are you when no one knows you, no one cares about you, and no one's watching? Solo travel will show you. But in my experience, it's not as much fun as traveling with a friend.

WHO WANTS WHERE

What's more important to you: traveling to a specific country or traveling with a specific person?

If you're hellbent on a certain country, don't invite a friend to travel with you, acting like you want to choose a destination together. Avoid this conversation:

"What about Spain? I've always wanted to go to Spain."

"I've been there. I want to go someplace new."

"Gotcha. What aboouuutt...Morocco? It's super close to Spain."

"Ooohhh. Don't they have, like, monkeys and snakes there? In that one plaza? I do *not* like monkeys. But I *do* like deserts."

"Deserts...okayyy...I'm gonna throw something out there...let this simmer for a minute: what about... NAMIBIA?"

"Yaaasssssss."

And then you end up in Namibia (which, for the record, is one of my favorite countries). Except it's really more of an open-road adventure destination, and you were hoping for more of a European vibe. You wanted to take a train to that Moorish sword factory you heard about in Cádiz, track Hemingway in Madrid, and visit that Frank Gehry museum in Bilbao. You definitely wanted to go to Spain, not Namibia.

To open a jar, you need one hand anchoring the base and one hand twisting the lid. The all-too-common "What about [blank]?" method is like two hands trying to twist the same lid while neither holds the jar.

If you're not willing to compromise on a destination, be upfront about it by asking a friend or relative if they want to join you on your trip to Turkey or Turkmenistan. Sell them on your vision for the style and pace of the trip. Whoever you can successfully enroll is bound to be a better match anyway.

If you're committed to traveling with a specific person, be willing to make compromises about the destination to ensure you each get what you want out of the trip. If you or your companion feels lured in a direction you or they didn't want to go, both of you will suffer.

Choosing a travel companion and choosing a destination are tightly intertwined decisions. If your friend loves beaches, but your brother loves the rugged wilderness, make sure you go to Portugal with your friend and Mongolia with your brother, not the other way around.

A destination-first approach to choosing a travel companion isn't necessarily wrong. It's just a little selfish. Don't stubbornly insist on a particular destination unless you're prepared to go alone.

A companion-first approach to choosing a destination is far more diplomatic but increases the odds of inaction. Saying, "We should travel together" to your friend is like saying, "We should hang out sometime!" and then fifteen years go by and you haven't even gotten coffee once.

Have a bias for action.

Under Consideration

My favorite travel style is the equivalent of Bruce Lee's fighting style: the style that eschews styles. As soon as you adhere to a particular label, you trap yourself in a box, and the style to which you claim to adhere controls you.

Of course, every traveler has preferred lenses through which they experience a new place, whether it be food, history, art, architecture, sports, music, or fashion. Some people are beach fiends, some are shopaholics, and some go in search of the most immersive and authentic cultural encounters they can find.

You don't have to choose labels to define the type of traveler you are or the focus of your trip. You shouldn't. But it is helpful to ponder the relative weight of your interests and preferred modes of exploration.

- How physically active do you want to be in your destination?
- How much time do you want to devote to relaxation and renewal?
- How much of your time do you want to spend in cities versus small towns and villages?
- What's your preferred pace? How fast are you willing or able to move? Are you willing to adopt a more leisurely tempo if it means forgoing certain attractions?
- Do you have dietary restrictions that might make it hard to reach a fundamental level of comfort on which you are unwilling to compromise?

These considerations demand of you no conformity to any movement, dogma, or trend. Get clear about your preferences and you'll naturally narrow down your choice.

DISCOMFORT ZONE

If you've never traveled internationally before and you want to take a trip to India, prepare to be shocked.

Even experienced travelers are overwhelmed by India's sensory explosion. But the perceived exoticism of a place is dictated by our past travel experiences. And the more exotic a place is to us, the more confronting it will be.

Think of it like a swimming pool. Which end of the pool will you jump into? Shallow, deep, or somewhere in the middle? It depends how good of a swimmer you are—and how daring you are.

Getting out of your comfort zone isn't a tangential benefit of international travel; it's the reason to do it. Exactly how far out of your comfort zone you want to go (and how abruptly you're willing to get there) is up to you. It's a very important choice.

(If it's an English-speaking country, you're still in the shallow end.)

There is no wrong or more noble choice here, only the right one for you at this time.

Challenging trips that require greater sacrifices of creature comforts may yield a heightened sense of post-trip triumph. But during the trip, your patience, bowels, lungs, and instincts will be tested.

Work your way up to spicier destinations. If you're "between sizes," opt for the riskier option. Never be reckless or sacrifice your safety. If you jump into the deep end before you're ready, start to drown, and need to be rescued, then you may never go swimming again. That would be unfortunate.

AT ALL COSTS

A getaway can be a budget adventure, a luxury affair, or anything in between. The important thing is to get real about what level of extravagance you can afford.

You can take a budget trip in an expensive country, but it's a lot harder. Even if you take a road trip in Iceland, you're still going to have to pay $6.50/gallon for gas. A McDonald's Big Mac meal costs $12 in Denmark; imagine what a three-course meal at a proper restaurant will run you.

Choose a destination that is generally well-matched for your budget.

First, figure out the maximum amount you can spend on the whole trip, including flights and accommodation. After that, set a rough daily budget for food and fun.

The potentially high cost of getting to an affordable destination, like Vietnam or Madagascar, may offset its budget appeal. The potentially low cost of getting to a pricey destination, like Iceland, may keep it within striking distance (although I would probably take a shuttle for the forty-minute ride from the airport into Reykjavik instead of a taxi, which will run you a cool $220).

WEATHER-WISE

Before my sister and I decided to travel to Japan together in April 2016, it was already high on my shortlist as a destination that aligned with my travel goals. I wanted a balanced blend of immersive cultural experiences, dining and shopping in one of the most electric cities on earth, a spiritual component, colorful and diverse photography opportunities, and quality bonding time with my sister.

Once my sister and I determined that April worked well with each of our schedules, Japan became the irrefutable winner. Early April is peak cherry blossom season, one of the most coveted times to see Japan in full bloom.

If you're drooling over Morocco's vibrant cities but can only travel in midsummer, it's probably best to avoid the broiling heat and save Morocco for another time.

If you don't care enough about the weather to let it dictate your choice of destination, allow me to share my Tahiti story.

RAINY SEASON IN TAHITI

The resort would have been lovely, but it was the rainy season. The general mood of all guests was self-piteous and resigned. I had no idea who else was staying at the property until dinner beckoned everyone out of their bungalows.

We borrowed umbrellas to keep us dry on the trot from dock to lobby. I thought the gale force winds might sweep me up like Mary Poppins and catapult me into the South Pacific, but the rental umbrellas were far too flimsy for even a hint of functionality. Within seconds after stepping out of the bungalow, they inverted, catching water in their wiry cones while exposing the holder to an onslaught of horizontal rain.

Instead of wrestling with the umbrellas, most guests resorted to using them as shields, bracing themselves against the storm as if holding a giant pad against which a practitioner of tae kwon do might perfect his or her roundhouse kick technique.

The stress of merely choosing whether or not to use an umbrella, thus volunteering myself for the wrangling, soaking, and tiresome self-defense the choice entailed, kept me staunchly stationed in the anti-umbrella camp. If I could have had access to the buffet without leaving the bungalow, I probably would have stayed inside for five straight days.

Swimming didn't look too appealing. The water was choppy and ominous, and I don't find stingrays to be the most amicable underwater companions. Stand-up paddle boarding wasn't even on the menu.

CHAPTER 3

The sun became my god. Whenever I detected a change in the light, however slight, I burst through the sliding doors onto our deck, stepping onto the second beam of the wood railing to get a closer look, waiting for the clouds to part. If any suggestion of a shadow appeared, I squinted in premature anticipation of the flood of holy light that would at any moment pour down onto me. I used my hand as a visor to protect my eyes from the imminent celestial splendor, a burning, blinding, blissful answer to my imploring prayers. It was as if I had lit an SOS fire and, on the brink of demise, heard a plane propeller overhead, come at last to rescue me. For most of a full day, I was the island's prisoner and the sky's puppet. It toyed with me, teasing me with momentary blasts of brightness. I responded on strings, scurrying back outside, head craned toward a still-gray abyss of ruined vacation, spinning in dizzying circles, stumbling like a summer camper finishing a relay race.

When the sun finally came out, I was determined to celebrate the occasion in the water. My wife, Annie, acquiesced when I implored her to lather my back with sunscreen, but instead of joining me, she opted to read a magazine on the deck of our bungalow. I prematurely put on my flippers and stomped through the mud toward the reef's most strategic entry point.

In the channel between the motu and the nearest islet, the water was shallow, barely over ten feet at its deepest point, but with bushels of coral polyps billowing up to the surface. Factoring in a formidable river-like current and the totality of coral coverage in the channel, it was tiring work to stay buoyant while dodging the underwater architecture.

Even while floating on my chest, the current carried and twirled me into elaborate coral empires. Trying to avoid

54

standing on the intricate structures, I resorted to fluttering my forearms like a wounded manatee, attempting to steer rather than swim, which there simply was not enough space to do given the shallowness, patchiness, and jaggedness of the terrain.

The marine life was decent, but I could barely appreciate the tropical fish for a few seconds before being swept away in what felt like a mini riptide. Cursing myself inside my mask, I vowed to control my movements and relax in one spot long enough to say "wow" and mean it.

I was pulled into an obstacle course of coral. Just then, I noticed a massive, synchronized school of shimmering minnows. Emboldened by this discovery and eager to move closer, I performed a frantic underwater hula dance, propelling myself into a deeper pocket of water with only sand underneath. I paused there and floated calmly in an upright position, but the school of minnows faded like a distant black cloud.

Making one final effort to chase them, another rush of riptide spun me back into the sharp formations. My toes, exposed through the tips of my flippers, grazed an unruly polyp, and the skin on my middle-right toe knuckle ripped off, which stung like a diabolical jellyfish and left a wisp of blood trailing off my foot like smoke from an exploded firework.

I announced my resolution to "fuck this coral" before standing up on an especially colorful and certainly sensitive chunk of it, home to myriad exotic eels, blowfish, urchins, and baby sharks. This sent creatures and vegetation alike into a spin cycle, creating a small typhoon peppered with murdered clams and enraged barracudas.

I managed to stand up and remove my mask, draining the salt water that had been filling it up to my lower eyelids.

Hyperventilating like an obese aquatic moose, with my goggles dangling on my ear like a bandage, not to mention my gushing foot, I was done snorkeling.

I carried my flippers back to the kiosk, depleted. My back felt crispy. When I flopped into the bungalow, Annie looked up from the magazine she was still reading to ask, "What the hell happened to you?"

The sun had been all I could think about; I yearned for it, dreamed of it, begged for it—and my desperation had doomed me. In my frantic rush to get into the water, I left no time for the lotion to absorb.

The next morning, I could barely get out of bed. My back was riper than a pineapple. Every pore sizzled. I was scorched from my hairline to my waist—a dark red, horrific burn that crept over my shoulders onto the backs of my arms. I looked like a raw tuna steak.

Any twisting or bending reignited the blaze, but what stung even more than the sunburn was the realization that I had managed to get so blisteringly burned in the only thirty-minute stretch of sun in nine days of torrential misery.

Before you book your trip to paradise, check the forecast.

ENDANGERED PLACES

Places threatened by climate change or over-tourism are always at the top of my travel list. If diving on the Great Barrier Reef is at the top of your bucket list, do it ASAP because the reef may soon be dead.

In Antarctica (and Montana and Switzerland and just about everywhere else), glaciers are receding at alarming rates. Penguin

populations are plummeting. In forty years, the Antarctic Peninsula may not exist.

Personally, the biggest factor in the way I choose destinations
is tourism. One of the toughest balancing acts in travel is picking
a destination that is neither too remote nor too trampled. On the
remote end of the spectrum, there's Siberia, vast and untapped. On
the trampled end of the spectrum, there's Machu Picchu, which
had to cap its daily allowed visitors at 2,500 (down from 5,000).

Anyplace that imposes visitor maximums raises a red flag. Does
that mean you should never visit Machu Picchu? Maybe. If you
rushed to Machu Picchu now, before it's "ruined" forever, you'd
only be contributing to the speed of its demise.

You need to weigh the degree to which you feel called to a place
with its degree of endangerment. Ask yourself, if this place no
longer existed in ten years, would I forever regret not going while
I had the chance?

Machu Picchu will still exist in ten years, and it will still be
glorious. But it will be worse than it is today. Mass tourism will
wear it down even more. I fear for this inevitable outcome because
I had the privilege of visiting Machu Picchu in 1999, on one of my
earliest international family vacations.

HAVE YOUR MACHU AND PICCHU, TOO

We stayed at the Sanctuary Lodge. Back then, the lodge
offered its guests a five-dollar add-on option to their daytime Machu Picchu entry tickets to reenter the ruins at night.
Today, the Sanctuary Lodge is a Belmond luxury property.
Twenty years ago, it was a small inn with basic rooms and few
guests. When night fell, we walked a hundred feet to the entry

gate, flashed our tickets at the guard, and he swung open Machu Picchu's front door for my family. Wonder-struck, we roamed the moonlit ruins in spooky silence. When we'd sufficiently soaked in Machu's mystical aura, we found our way back to the gate and hollered at the guard to let us out. We could have slept in there if we wanted to.

Can you imagine having Machu Picchu all to yourself today?

The government shut down night tours a decade ago to prevent further erosion. But that's certainly not the only thing that's changed about the World Wonder since I was there.

The next morning, my dad and I woke up at dawn and summited Huayna Picchu, Machu Picchu's iconic backdrop peak. We were the only people on the trail—a trail that has since been completely rebuilt. In 1999, the summit was merely a stack of boulders, one of which had a plaque on it. Now there's a lookout platform big enough to hold thirty people and a 400-person daily limit on the trail.

The hike is still just as steep and vertigo-inducing as it was when I climbed, and I assume the reinforced trail is more robust. But the sheer volume of people on the trail at any given time, hugging the stones on one side of the narrow staircase to avoid falling into the Peruvian abyss on the other, would make me think twice about attempting to tag the summit. Not only does it seem more dangerous now (I may never return to find out for sure), but I imagine the transcendent solitude I experienced on the summit is impossible to re-create. My thirteen-year-old mind was blown.

I don't mean to discredit arguably the most marvelous attraction on earth. I encourage people to see World Wonders with their own eyes whenever and however they can. They've earned their fame, and visitors derive an ineffable satisfaction from witnessing them—walking on the Great Wall of China, exploring Angkor Wat, standing in the shadow of Christ the Redeemer in Rio de Janeiro.

But these places are just as endangered as the ice in Antarctica. Despite the best efforts to preserve them, trampled, overcrowded tourist hotspots are constantly deteriorating. If you can resist their spell, go somewhere undiscovered instead. Find the new Machu Picchu and have it all to yourself.

THEME SONG

Trips aren't just about exploring places. They're about exploring ideas.

Choosing a theme for your trip will unify your activities. A theme is the lens through which you'll view your destination.

Perhaps you're a sustainability aficionado seeking a green trip with a conservation bent. You could stay only at carbon-negative properties and avoid *flygskam* (flight shame) by traversing the Atlantic in a sailboat.

Maybe you're a wellness fiend seeking a deep dive into fitness and health. You belong at a spa in Gstaad, exfoliating in volcanic mud after a sound therapy session.

Or you're a gastronomy guru, determined to taste the essence of your destination. Your trip will be a series of gustatory indulgences and culinary discoveries, featuring locally sourced produce prepared by the world's top chefs.

Are you an athlete? Design a physically challenging trip to train while you travel. Trekking in Nepal? Cycling in the Dolomites?

There are so many more themes to choose from: pet-friendly travel, train travel, conscious luxury, spartan minimalism. If you design your trip around a core value system, make sure your commitment to those values comes from within and is not motivated by a fleeting desire to abide by momentary trends.

DONE DEAL

Choosing a destination only because it's a good deal is like accepting a job only for the money. It won't leave you feeling fulfilled.

Deal sites like Scott's Cheap Flights can be extremely beneficial for finding flight bargains. Just be careful not to let the allure of the deal mar the purpose you've declared for your trip and the dates that work for you.

Since flash deals are limited to specific date ranges, you may be tempted by a destination—even one on your shortlist—but the dates don't align with the window in which you were hoping to travel. That's not a good deal.

Only jump on limited-time deals if all elements match the vision and goals you've outlined. If the destination is one of the three on your shortlist, and the timing is perfect, and the price is right, by all means, grab it!

Bon Voyage

I assume you're not planning a getaway because a potato blight ravaged your country and forced you to flee to avoid starvation. But I know you have your reasons. Identify your trip's purpose, and you will happen to it, rather than letting it happen to you.

Choose the travel companion the trip needs, not just the first friend you think of whose schedule is clear.

Take your trip at the right time. Try not to visit paradise during hurricane season. Wait at least fifteen minutes after you apply sunscreen to go snorkeling.

Clarify your budget, pick your pace, and specify the lens you'll be looking through. Tread the deepest water you can.

There is no objective master list of the "best" countries to visit. Do your best to select the destination most likely to light you up.

Have you chosen? Well, then…

It's time to tackle tickets.

CHAPTER 4

Flight School

"From this hour I ordain myself loos'd of limits and
imaginary lines,
Going where I list, my own master total and absolute."
—WALT WHITMAN

BOOKING FLIGHTS IS intimidating. It's the first and usually the most expensive purchase you make in the travel process. Once you book flights, you have real skin in the game. It's on.

As airlines make concessions and travelers become more discerning, a strategy of careful optimism may take some pain out of the flight-booking experience.

This chapter covers where and how to book flights without getting sucker punched by tempting deals that turn out to be money traps or booking a route that eats up half your travel days with layovers and delays.

Your trip is a sandwich, and your flights are the bread. If that bread is too soggy, or too crusty, or too thin, or too thick, it can ruin your whole sandwich. Here's how to achieve toasty perfection.

Get to the Points

There are countless blogs about points and miles, credit cards, and "travel hacking." You can get as extreme as you want with it. Some obsessive travel hackers juggle over ten credit cards, jump on every bonus, and finesse the system to fly in business or first class, anywhere in the world, for free. These pros have developed elaborate spending systems to accrue gobs of points and redeem them for maximum value.

You don't need an elaborate system, but you do need a strategy. To be effective, it must be simple. If it's too complicated, you could screw up your credit, pay excessive annual fees, and waste a lot of time and energy for minimal net gain.

Your goal should be to earn as many points as possible without changing what you buy. You only need to change where and how you buy. Let your existing spending habits dictate your strategy. Look for the low-hanging fruit of miles-earning potential. Set up recurring payments with the highest grossing card you have for all of your bills.

Many airlines, hotels, and credit card companies have their own shopping portals. Use them. Infrequent but significant purchases like printer ink and contact lenses often have sizable bonuses. Visit evreward.com to see which reward portal is offering the highest bonus for any given merchant.

You can also earn points the old-fashioned way: by flying. Set up accounts with airlines you fly often. Confirm that you received miles you already earned. Most airlines will retroactively credit you for flights flown within the last year.

COUNTING CARDS

Just as there's no "best" destination, there's no "best" card either.

The best card for you is the one that provides the most value to you right now. Here's my starting lineup:

- I use the **Amex Platinum Card** to get five times the points when I book flights. (When I do pay cash, this bonus dampens the sting.)
- I use the **Amex Gold Card** to get four times the points at grocery stores and restaurants. (I put some serious damage on this card during peak Rona season, when grocery shopping became a heart-racing adventure.)
- I use the **Chase Ink Business Preferred** to get three times the points on travel (hotels, car rentals, ferries, etc.), shipping, and advertising costs.
- I use the **Chase Ink Business Plus** to get five times the points at office supply stores, and on my internet and phone bill, plus double the points at gas stations.
- I use the **Chase Freedom Unlimited** to get 1.5 times the points on everything else.
- And I use Bitcoin when I buy Bugattis in Abu Dhabi.

DOUBLE-DIPPING

In a nontravel context, I'm anti-gift card. You forget to use them, then they stack up in your kitchen drawer, then four years go by, and you have no idea what any of the balances are. Besides, are you ever going to eat at Applebee's?

But for points acquisition, gift cards are one of the most brilliant hacks in the game.

It's simple. You buy gift cards at a store (for example, a grocery or office supply store) with a credit card that pays high bonuses at that type of store. Then you spend the gift card on whatever it's for (ideally immediately). This allows you to earn bonus points on purchases beyond those included in your credit card perks.

For example, the Chase Ink Business Plus card pays five times the points at office supply stores. Guess what office supply stores sell? Amazon gift cards. I make the occasional trip to Office Depot, walk out with a pocketful of Amazon moolah, scan all the barcodes into my Amazon account before I leave the parking lot, and effectively earn five times the points on everything I buy on Amazon.

This double-dipping technique is far less uncouth than redipping the mouth-facing side of a half-munched Tostitos chip into the guacamole bowl at a Super Bowl party.

CHECKS AND BALANCES

Streamlining your systems for earning points, in accordance with your spending habits, is essential for anyone hoping to make travel more comfortable, convenient, and affordable. But many travelers have no idea how many miles they have, let alone how to use them strategically. Booking flights should always start with an appraisal of your points and miles balances.

AwardWallet is a helpful service for tracking all of your balances in one place. The pro version of the itinerary management tool, TripIt, also includes a handy points-tracker feature.

The goal is to understand how your existing points could be utilized or combined to pay, at least partially, for your flights.

Look up your mileage programs' transfer partners. Pay attention to overlapping transfer partners from different programs. For example, if you have some points on American Express and some on Chase Ultimate Rewards, you could transfer points from each of them to Emirates or Virgin Atlantic to pay for a flight you didn't have enough to cover with only one account.

Every time I reassess my travel account balances, I'm pleasantly surprised. Sometimes it's because I realize I was credited for miles I passively earned on flights I forgot I took. Sometimes it's because I realize my points are transferrable to an airline I never considered flying on before, which happens to be perfect for the trip I'm planning.

Know your numbers.

REDEEM YOURSELF

To maximize the value of your points, always compare redemption options on your bank's points portal and with airline transfer partners.

Transferring points is usually a better value but not always.

Booking through a portal can be a better option than transferring points in certain situations (in economy class), for example:

- If the airline you want to fly is not a transfer partner of the portal where you have points.
- If saver awards are limited or nonexistent (which, with the popularity of dynamic award prices, they often are).
- If your specific credit card increases the value of your points when you book directly on a portal—for example, 1.25 cents per point with the Chase Sapphire Preferred or 1.5 cents per point with the Chase Sapphire Reserve (rather than the usual 1 cent per point).
- If you want to earn redeemable mileage or status credit for the reservation. (You can't earn points on award tickets booked directly with airlines.)

Since portals' price redemptions are at a fixed rate, never book premium cabin redemptions on a portal.

Remember, points transfers are irreversible. Before you make a transfer, double-check the exchange ratio (almost always one-to-one) and the flight availability.

Don't shop with points. Earn points by shopping, and then redeem those points for flights (or hotels). Utilizing programs like Amazon's Shop with Points may seem like a convenient way to save, but you'll get lousy value.

Flying High

Layovers don't have to be painful (more on that in Chapter 11). Even a single, short, strategically utilized layover can make getting to your destination feel like a marathon, especially if you have to change terminals or go through security again. Follow these rules to optimize your route.

ONE-STOP SHOP

In 2019, Qantas Airlines tested ultra-long-haul, nineteen-hour flights from NYC and London to Sydney on Boeing 787-9s. With aviation technology advancing and new international routes making previously unthinkable routes possible, reaching your destination in two flights—with only one connection—is hardly an outrageous demand.

Depending on your home city and the remoteness of your destination, this may not be possible. For example, when I flew from Seattle to the British Virgin Islands, it took three flights: Seattle to Miami, Miami to Puerto Rico, and Puerto Rico to Virgin Gorda in a ten-seat Cessna 402. Sometimes two connections is the only way.

Travelers usually underestimate the cost of connections—not the monetary cost but the toll that an additional layover takes on their body, mood, and itinerary. They choose affordability over convenience. Which one you prioritize is your choice. But if you can stomach the price difference of a more convenient route that saves you an unnecessary layover, take the better route over the bargain.

If you were leaving the country for a month, it wouldn't matter so much if it took you seven extra hours to get there. On a shorter getaway, every hour counts.

If I'm trying to get from Seattle to Tashkent, Uzbekistan, obeying the **One-Connection Rule,** I can connect in Dubai, London, Seoul, or even New York City. Perhaps I could save some money by taking three flights, connecting in Frankfurt and then Istanbul before finally reaching Tashkent. That would only be worth it if it significantly cut back my total route duration. No, thanks. I want to *be* there for as long as possible and be getting there for as short as possible.

Everyone says the journey is the destination. Hot take: the destination is the destination.

GO LONG

Whenever I'm taking an international trip that requires two flights, I invoke the **Long-Flight-First Rule.** The first flight I take out of my home city should, ideally, be the longest one. With my first flight, I want to get as close to my final destination as possible.

For example, when I fly from Seattle to Athens, my best options are flying from Seattle to Newark to Athens, or from Seattle to Frankfurt to Athens. The Frankfurt option is much more appealing because with that routing, my long flight (ten hours) from Seattle to Frankfurt will be my first flight, and my short flight (three hours) will come second.

Why does this matter? It's going to take the same amount of time to get there regardless.

Psychologically, long flights take a toll. They're bigger mental hurdles. Imagine stepping off a six-hour flight, still being in the same country, with a three-hour connection in Newark, and another eight-hour flight still in front of you. By the time you board that second flight, you'll feel like you're twenty-two miles into the Athens marathon.

On the other hand, if you step off a ten-hour flight in Frankfurt, also a sweaty mess, but can say, "Okay, we're in Germany! Just a few more hours to Greece," you'll feel a greater sense of progress and excitement.

One possible exception to the Long-Flight-First Rule is if the first flight is extremely short. For example, if there were a direct flight from Vancouver to Athens (there's not), I'd happily fly from Seattle to Vancouver (one hour) to take it.

Sometimes just getting out of the United States with my first flight, even if the shorter leg does come first, feels like a psychological victory. Although there is no flight from Vancouver to Athens, there is one from Toronto to Athens. Seattle to Toronto takes four and a half hours. I'd rather get to Europe with my first leg, but if for some reason that's not possible, I'd prefer a connection in Toronto over one in Newark.

Always consider the order of your flights and your connecting airport. You have options!

Advanced Booking

I booked a flight from London to Tashkent, Uzbekistan on Expedia. The Uzbekistan Airlines website was glitchy and hard to decipher; I thought Expedia would be more dependable.

Then COVID happened, and I remembered why booking with an Online Travel Agency (OTA) is never a good idea.

I spent three months trying to get a refund from Expedia. I won't elaborate on the agony I suffered. Suffice it to say, I wouldn't wish a fraction of that pain on my most insipid foe. Finally, I gave up and filed a dispute with my credit card provider. After another month, I got my refund.

I'm not sure getting a refund directly from Uzbekistan Airlines would have been much easier, but the fiasco made me wonder, is it *ever* better to book flights with an OTA?

THIRD-PARTY FOULS

Sometimes flights may indeed be cheaper on an OTA. But unless they are drastically cheaper (which they hardly ever are) and unless you're absolutely positive that absolutely nothing about your reservation will change (which you can hardly ever be), the slightly cheaper prices you may find won't come close to offsetting the following blatant disadvantages of booking anywhere other than directly with the airline:

- Communicating with OTAs is flat-out inconvenient. Flight changes or cancellations are excruciating to sort out. The customer service sucks.
- Refunds can take months, if you're able to get them at all.
- Third-party booking services direct you to the airline to deal with any issues. The airline's response is usually, "You didn't book it with us, so it's not our problem."
- Reserving seats on an OTA is a nuisance. You likely won't be able to do so at the time of purchase and will have to go to the airline's website anyway. Only then might you find out there is no available adjacent pair, and you and your travel companion will have to sit fifteen rows apart, both in middle seats.

- You may still be able to earn loyalty points when you book on an OTA. But you won't be able to redeem any points you may have available for a particular airline.
- Low-cost airlines don't always appear on OTAs, so the results you're seeing could be far from comprehensive.
- Some airlines, like Lufthansa, charge fees for booking with OTAs.
- It can take up to forty-eight hours for the OTA to issue your ticket. After all, when you book via OTA, you're not buying a ticket; you're merely requesting that the OTA reserves your ticket. They may then tell you the flight isn't available or isn't available at the price you tried to buy it at. They may not honor the impossibly cheap "mistake fare" deal you were pumping your fist about yesterday.
- The US Department of Transportation mandates that airlines allow tickets to be canceled free of charge within twenty-four hours of booking. OTAs likely offer similar cancellation protection, but they're not required to and may not.
- You may think booking multi-airline itineraries with bundled add-ons in the same transaction is the pinnacle of convenience, until you realize you have a twenty-five-minute connection in Munich, which is barely enough time to queue for a bratwurst. On OTAs, impossibly short connections often go unflagged.
- Flights may appear cheaper on OTAs, but there are often airline-imposed surcharges and high cancellation/change fees that negate the value of the affordable fare.

Booking directly with the airline is vastly simpler and more convenient. Use third parties like Expedia, Orbitz, and Priceline to browse, and then buy directly on the airline's site.

CHEAP THRILLS

If you can't use points to book flights, smart shopping for airfare makes all the difference.

The more flexible you are with your dates, the more likely you are to find affordable flights. A mid-week departure, for example, could save you hundreds of dollars compared to a Saturday morning flight. The day of the week on which you book your flight has less bearing on its price than your departure date does.

Try to book two to six or even up to eight months in advance for the best rates and availability.

Budget carriers can be tempting, but if you insist on using one, be careful. Not only are the planes uncomfortable, but those carriers love to slap you with extra fees for meals, bags, seats...I wouldn't be surprised if they started charging a dollar every time you lowered your tray table.

Flight deal newsletters like Scott's Cheap Flights or Airfare Watchdog are useful as a passive strategy, but perfect deals, like rare orchids, are hunted. Scott's Cheap Flights sends alerts about mistake fares, but they usually disappear before the incredulous expression on your face does.

Flight metasearch sites (specifically Google Flights, Skyscanner, and Momondo) are the best places to start looking.

Google Flights has the cleanest interface and a handy flexible dates feature. It's nice to be able to search for a region rather than a specific city and explore prices for destinations in the vicinity of your target. Flying to alternate airports could help you save, as could adding a short connecting flight to avoid flying directly to a more expensive city.

Skyscanner, a perennial favorite, sweeps the internet for the cheapest rates possible. It also has a flexible dates feature (click on departure date, then choose "Whole Month" instead of "Specific

Date"), and it lets you "Get Price Alerts" (look for the bell icon). It then redirects you to an airline or OTA (uh-uh, honey) to finalize your booking. Skyscanner tends to catch fares from smaller and potentially cheaper OTAs than Google Flights, which could save you a few bucks if you insist on disregarding my impassioned OTA diatribe above (I pray you won't). These obscure travel agencies should have a "Proceed with Caution" sticker next to the "Select" button.

Momondo is another respectable tool to check, with an Explore map like Google Flights'. Like most of its counterparts, Momondo lets you mix and match airlines to find the cheapest route.

I love the idea of booking individual flight legs separately to save money or book a more favorable route, but booking a multi-flight, multi-carrier itinerary with some wet-noodle OTA spells disaster. Imagine calling CheapOAir to explain that your first flight on Frontier was delayed, which caused you to miss your second flight on Spirit. How do you think that conversation will go?

ENTER THE MATRIX

Booking flights is more complicated than inputting a departure city, an arrival city, and some dates. Each flyer has their own preferences and pet peeves, airports they love or loathe, airlines or alliances to which they profess allegiance, perhaps even certain models of aircrafts they either swear by or detest. Metasearch juggernaut Google Flights is very helpful but not as comprehensive as the software that drives it—ITA Flight Matrix.

ITA Matrix is the granddaddy of flight metasearch. Unlike an OTA, it does not allow you to book flights directly through the service. Rather, it redirects you to airlines' sites to book.

The specificity of search parameters makes ITA Matrix the single most useful flight-booking tool. You can filter and sort to find flights based on what is most important to you. I usually start by sorting results by number of stops, unchecking options with two or more. I then sort by duration to view the shortest routes.

Of course, you can sort by price instead. But I like to take a best-case-scenario approach and find the dreamiest, most convenient itinerary available and then see if I can reverse engineer it. If the shortest one-stop itinerary is prohibitively expensive and on an airline I've never heard of, at least I'll know that it exists. I can then reassess my points and miles balances and check if that airline is a transfer partner of any of my source accounts.

ITA Matrix also lets you filter results by specific connection airports or plane types. It sometimes shows flights on small or obscure airlines that other metasearches don't catch. These flights can make all the difference in finessing the perfect itinerary.

Third-party OTAs and metasearch engines sometimes show flight results with layovers as short as twenty-five minutes. You might find a crazy cheap deal, but the layover time is just not practical. In the Matrix, you can specify minimum layover times to make sure the connection is feasible. It also warns you about red eyes and long or risky connections.

The true value of the ITA Matrix is that it allows you to see everything in one place.

The link is matrix.itasoftware.com.

FINE PRINT

Don't rush through the checkout process when you're buying flights. The details matter. Triple-check dates, arrival and departure times, baggage allowances, even the spelling of your own name. Add your Known Traveler Number (KTN) if you have one (you do, if you have TSA PreCheck or Global Entry). And as tedious as it may be, read the fine print. You always have twenty-four hours to cancel a ticket (to the minute—don't take any chances), but you may need to pay to change your reservation (here's hoping COVID killed change fees forever). Either way, the airline may still charge you for fare differences. Make sure you understand the policies you're agreeing to and not checking any boxes you don't mean to check.

Booking flights requires the pouncing instinct of a cheetah and the vigilance of the gazelle it hunts. Stay sharp to escape the flight savanna unscathed.

Please Be Seated

You're not done booking flights until you have a seat—a seat you can live with and might actually be comfortable in.

If, for any reason, you're unable to view or choose seats before you pay, pump the brakes. Call the airline to ensure that your preferred seat or seat type is available. Never just hope that you don't get put in a middle seat.

Once you're positive you won't be pigeonholed into seat 36E, which happens to be broken and doesn't recline, with rancid lavatory odors wafting over you, you're safe to book your flight. In most cases, you will be able to pick your seat in the checkout process but not always. If you're booking far in advance, it may be too early.

Take this approach: if you don't have a seat, you don't have a flight.

Reserving not-horrible seats usually costs money on most major airlines. Airlines have their own heat maps. They know exactly which seats are the most popular, and they want you to pay for them.

The seat you select is up to you, and if you're confident you'll be comfortable in a free seat, fantastic. But no matter what, choose one. Never let the airline assign you a seat. This is like going to a restaurant and saying, "Bring me whatever," and then complaining when you get a can of clams with 20 percent gratuity included.

FIRST CHAIR

If choosing a seat were as simple as "window or aisle?" then **SeatGuru** wouldn't exist.

Read seat reviews from previous passengers who learned the hard way that they had that one weird window seat with a wall instead of a window. Find out in advance if the tray table is in the armrest of the seat you're considering, or if the proximity to the bassinets negates the extra legroom of a bulkhead seat. If the bulkhead barrier is just a flimsy curtain, you won't be able to rest your heels on the folded-over tops of the magazines protruding out of the wall-mounted pouch.

Pay close attention to the plane's seating configuration. What's the layout? Two-four-two? Three-three-three? Ten abreast: three-four-three?

Snagging twin seats is a huge score when you're flying with a companion. If flying economy, I always try to grab a two-seat row, and sometimes I choose my flight based on the availability of open pairs.

Some planes with three-three-three or three-four-three configurations do have some rows with only two seats. Not surprisingly, they're among the most expensive economy seats you can pick. A smooth move if you're booking an award ticket in economy is to pay cash to upgrade to one of these "private" rows, if any are available. Sharing a row exclusively with your travel buddy is the closest you can get to business class. Besides, rubbing Rona shoulders with strangers is *so* 2019.

Seat alerts from **Expert Flyer** can be especially useful for frequent fliers or travelers hoping to score a specific seat on a specific flight. It's like Craigslist—rudimentary interface yet extremely useful. The free membership notifies you if a better seat becomes available. The basic membership for $4.99 per month lets you search for award and upgrade availability, which could easily pay for itself if it helps you find a cheap award on a favorable route. The premium membership for $9.99 per month or $99.99 per year will alert you when your preferred flights become available, so you don't have to keep checking back.

SIT BACK, RELAX

Choosing seats on international flights (your trip's sandwich bread, remember?) is much more important than choosing seats on domestic flights. If your trip is only nine days, for example, you don't want to spend one of those days praying flight attendants don't spill ginger ale on you and agonizing over simple yet somehow difficult questions like, "Chicken or pasta?"

Beyond price and placement, also consider your own priorities, body, and in-flight tendencies:

- How do you sleep on planes?
- Are you tall? Are you wide?
- Will you have a tight connection when you land and benefit from sitting closer to the front so you can deboard quicker?
- Are you going to work on the flight or watch three *Mission Impossibles* just to find the scene where Tom Cruise runs down the side of the Burj Khalifa, only to realize that scene

was in none of the three mediocre action films you just snoozed through, but whatever, it's all good?

- Will you need quick and regular access to your 40 L "personal item," which obviously doesn't fit below the seat in front of you and contains your precious supply of dark chocolate that you want to keep close but not too close, so you don't eat the whole bar before you take off?

- Will choosing a window seat mean you dehydrate yourself to avoid having to tap your slumbering row mate to let you sneak out three to five times on your long-haul flight, which deep down you know is totally reasonable because everybody has to pee on planes, and it's not that big of a deal but still?

- What's your bigger nightmare: crying babies (proximity to bassinets) or wafting stenches (proximity to lavatories)? How much was first class again?

Floating on Air

It baffles me how little commercial airplane cabin interiors, especially in economy class, have changed in the past fifty years. The gross upholstery. The flimsy cushions. The sardine-can seating and awkward armrest wrangling. Not surprisingly, millions of passengers have come to accept that flying is a detestable experience every time. Assuming inevitable in-flight discomfort makes booking tickets even more stressful. Flyers are rightfully unenthused about the product they're buying. Buying and taking flights feel like chores, which makes the entire trip feel like a chore, which is tragic.

Pulling back the points and miles curtain, you begin to see through the aviation industry's casual duplicity. You realize the extent to which airlines have gone to maintain the allure of their premium offerings. You remember that seat classes, upgrade eligibility, and the pomposity of champagne before takeoff (while Joe Schmo can't get a Minute Maid until we reach our cruising altitude) are flimsy emblems of status. Behind each curtain there are four more curtains. Beyond each retractable vinyl line divider there is another divided line. You need a private jet to keep from feeling like a third-class citizen. Just give me my damn pretzels.

But you can beat the airlines at their own games. Create a points strategy that rewards you handsomely for your existing spending habits. Use flight browsing and booking services to score the routes and seats you really want—not just the ones that will get the job done. It may take more time, patience, and discipline than you're accustomed to exerting. You may have to start your flight search earlier than you usually do to find nuggets of gold. Airlines are betting that you don't have the stamina for it. They've put their money on you gnawing peanuts and begging for a full can of V8 in seat 32B until the cows come home. The cows are currently in Bangladesh, and there has been a six-cow pileup in Rangpur causing quite a traffic jam. This could take a while.

Spit out the peanuts and drop the juice. Comfortable, affordable flights can be yours. Once you've cleared the flight hurdle, the real fun begins.

CHAPTER 5

The Art of
Itinerary Design

"We wander for distraction,
but we travel for fulfillment."
—HILAIRE BELLOC

I ONCE TOLD an acquaintance about my upcoming trip to Greece. I told her I had the whole thing dialed in and planned to perfection. I considered every detail. It was an airtight itinerary.

"When my husband and I went to Greece in the '80s," she said, "we just caught a ferry to wherever the next one happened to be going. It was totally spontaneous."

I wasn't jealous. Although open itineraries offer greater flexibility, that flexibility is more often a curse than a blessing. It works if you have unlimited time and nowhere to be, but not if your travel time is finite.

My parents also did some marauding in Greece in bygone decades. They once missed the last scheduled ferry out of Rhodes, ended up sleeping on the beach, and befriended a Greek couple whom they stayed in touch with for forty years.

Sure, it can be liberating to travel with no schedule, no rules, and no checkpoints. But improvising travelers inevitably pay a price for it. With no plans, you're more likely to make rash, chaotic decisions rather than calculated ones based on your genuine desires.

Put some elbow grease into your itinerary design so you don't wash up on another rocky shore every time Poseidon sneezes.

Cloud Nine

The impressively rotund and mustachioed twenty-seventh President of the United States, William Howard Taft, responded to a 1910 *New York Times* cover story that asked, in all caps, "HOW LONG SHOULD A MAN'S VACATION BE?"

Taft argued that his fellow Americans "ought to have a change of air where they can expand their lungs and get exercise in the open" before positing his official opinion on optimal annual leisure time: "two or three months' vacation…are necessary in order to continue work the next year with that energy and effectiveness which it ought to have."

Taft was onto something with his nod to the enduring value of leisure, but taking two months annual leave is not realistic for most Americans. Besides, I'm not inclined to endorse the opinion of a politician with a propensity for excess. According to Taft's housekeeper, he "wanted a thick, juicy twelve-ounce steak nearly every morning."

Most people would settle for a thick, juicy, long weekend. There's nothing wrong with a short trip or weekend getaway— they can be fun, relaxing, or romantic. In rarer cases, they can be transformative. But real transformation requires more time and a wider variety of immersive experiences.

You could take an extended trip instead—three weeks, a month, six months, or a year. You could quit your job, sell your car, rent out your home, hit the road, and "live the dream." You could become a vagabond.

But what if you don't want to quit your job? What if you're not prepared to make such weighty sacrifices? What if you have a thriving career and enjoy conquering your adult responsibilities?

There is a sweet spot: the 9-Day Getaway.

Two weekends and one business week. Time it with an official holiday, and you may need to take only a few days off work.

Science agrees. A study published in the *Journal of Happiness Studies* tracked the well-being of vacationers on summer holidays. The study found that well-being rapidly increases at the beginning of a vacation and peaks on the eighth day. That leaves one day for Dorothy to find her way home.

Any trip shorter than nine days runs the risk of being superficial. You blast through a place—you're *on* the place—but you're not really in it. It's not enough time to diversify your cultural, culinary, adventurous, spiritual, and educational experiences enough to say, "I'm going to remember that trip for the rest of my life." When you get home, you'll think, *I barely scratched the surface.*

In 2015, I spent five days in Iceland, gawking at volcanic landscapes. But because I was staying in the capital, Reykjavik, for all four nights, my exploration was limited to the southwest region of the country known as the Golden Circle. Many of Iceland's top attractions are located in this area, and I relished the novelty of touring a hydroponic tomato farm and exploring ice tunnels inside of a glacier. But I had limited encounters with local people, no variety in my accommodation, and could never seem to escape throngs of tour buses vying for space in geyser parking lots. Five days in Iceland is better than zero, but it wasn't long enough to sink all the way in and reach that rapturous moment when time becomes irrelevant.

Trips that push into the two- or three-week range run the opposite risk. Anxiety sets in when you feel your normal routine begin to unravel. A sense of disconnection follows. You become dangerously detached from your home life. You lose track of your obligations and start to float away into the euphoria of what you think is infinite freedom but what is closer to grand avoidance.

Of course, there's a value in prolonged periods of travel. You can sink into a place, learn its nuances and rhythms, and shed your preconceptions under its spell. But eventually, you'll have the "get me out of here" moment. You'll yearn for precisely what you once yearned to escape. When you come home, you'll have fond memories of your travels, but reintegrating into the nontravel mode could set you back mentally and emotionally.

That's what happened to me when I went to the World Cup in Brazil with two friends for eighteen days. The atmosphere was electric, but five cities and countless caipirinhas later, I felt like I had just run a marathon with a bushel of coconuts on my back. When I finally got home, the reverse culture shock had me dreaming in Portuguese and spontaneously screaming, "Gooooaaaalllll" on Wednesday afternoons in Seattle. It didn't help that on the last night of the trip, I'd eaten three pounds of meat at one of the best Brazilian steakhouses in Rio. There was some serious reverse stomach shock in the mix as well.

A nine-day trip is long enough to be immersive but short enough to force a healthy respect for the decided itinerary. You can see the finish line for the entirety of the race, but it's still far enough away that, at least sporadically, you forget you're racing.

When the trip ends, you're sad to leave but relieved to get home.

Your home life is waiting for you, right where you left it. You have a newfound perspective. You've recalibrated your priorities. You have stories to tell and reasons for telling them. You're inspired, rejuvenated, and supercharged.

That's the goal, isn't it?

Track Records

A trip itinerary is like a tourbillon watch, full of tiny moving parts. When the mechanism is complete, it's a thing of beauty. As it is being built, however, organizing its various springs and dials is no easy feat. Planning software simplifies the itinerary-building process.

GOOGLY-EYED

Google Trips disintegrated in 2019. Its fragments landed in other zip codes within the Google ecosystem. Google Flights, Hotels, and Maps work together as "Travel" at google.com/travel.

If you have a Google account, all of your past trips will automatically show up. Not creepy at all.

Since Google knows you better than you know yourself, the "Potential Trips" section may look like a bucket list-in-progress. "Things to Do" is a useful tool for browsing attractions.

The new Google Trips does simplify travel planning and organization, but I like it as a supplementary tool more than a comprehensive itinerary management tool.

It's not a risky decision to use it or not. Google is doing all the work for you anyway. Google Travel just lets you see it all in one place.

YOU MUST BE TRIPIT

Itinerary management software **TripIt** scans your email for hotel, car rental, and flight reservations and automatically organizes it all into one master, shareable itinerary. You can forward your confirmation emails to plans@tripit.com to make sure it doesn't miss anything.

TripIt's pro version for $49 per year is worth considering for anyone hoping to turn their getaways into routine occurrences. TripIt Pro offers a plethora of alerts and reminders regarding cancellations and delays, check-ins, gate changes, connections, baggage claim info, security wait estimates, and seat availability. Airline apps usually provide similar alerts, but TripIt Pro has more tricks up its sleeves: Point Tracker for managing airline and credit card reward accounts (useful in the trip planning phase but less relevant during travel), interactive airport maps, and country-specific info with currency conversion, socket and plug types, tipping etiquette, and embassy info. You may find these features scattered across other apps and tools, but TripIt unifies them.

A TripIt Pro account also gets you a discounted CLEAR membership and a one-time $25 LoungeBuddy credit (more on waltzing through security and inappropriate day drinking in Chapter 11).

<h3 style="text-align:center">WHAT'S UP, DOC?</h3>

Whereas Google Travel and TripIt create itineraries out of confirmed reservations, a Google Doc or Sheet is a living, breathing planning page, a hybrid itinerary and note page.

Start by creating a section or column for every day of your trip. Add comments about potential activities. Color-code what you've paid for already and what you still owe. Copy and paste blurbs from articles you read; whittle them down into small annotations as plans turn firm.

Add useful info you pull from guidebooks or websites: average costs, exchange rates, useful phrases, etiquette, anecdotes, or the expected price of a taxi from the airport to your hotel.

As your trip approaches, compare your itinerary to the one Google Travel or TripIt draws up for you. Your document will serve you best in the pre-trip phase, but TripIt may be simpler to refer to on travel days.

Good Nights

After booking flights, you'll be tempted to dive into all the fun activities available to you at your destination. That would be like building a house and, immediately after buying a plot of land, shopping for light fixtures.

The goal at this stage is to give structure to your itinerary. Work on nailing down the major components first.

The first question you need to answer is, in what city or town will I sleep each night of my trip?

You can't answer this question without first doing research—broad research. Learn the geography and topography of the country, its regions, provinces, national parks, and top attractions.

Maintain a macro perspective as you map out a rough itinerary. Guidebooks help at this stage, but it's too soon to choose restaurants and book tours. The biggest mistake people make in the early trip-planning stage is to become drunk on possibilities. We could go windsurfing! This hotel has a fifty-foot infinity pool! Ernest Hemingway sat on a stool here!

Stay focused on the question, Where will I sleep?

Pay attention to the locations of attractions that catch your eye on Pinterest or Instagram. If you're struggling to divvy up your nights, a higher concentration of saved spots on Google Maps may help you make a conclusive decision.

A backpacker on a yearlong, round-the-world trip doesn't need to devise a nightly plan with such exactitude, but you do.

ARTFUL THIEVERY

Tour companies create itineraries they believe will sell. These itineraries hit most or all of the main attractions in a given country or region.

The first thing you'll notice is that the trips are usually eight to nine days. Trips longer than that are harder to sell. Like you, these companies' target clients have busy lives and careers that aren't easy to abandon for two or more weeks.

The second thing you'll notice is that the itineraries are balanced to appeal to everyone. Perusing them will give you a sense of which attractions are unmissable and which are optional. You can then tailor your own itinerary to your own preferences, opting to spend more or less time in cities or rural areas or skip certain attractions that don't appeal to you to free up time for others that do.

Taking inspiration from preexisting itineraries is not theft. Inspiration is free; action is a premium.

The itineraries I create for myself overlap with, but are never identical to, premade itineraries. "Pretty good" isn't good enough. You deserve a bespoke fit.

PACE YOURSELF

Your nightly itinerary is tightly correlated with the pace of your trip. As a general rule, on a 9-Day Getaway, aim to divide the nights into three stays of two to three days each.

On a slower-paced trip, you may want to spend four nights in two spots. Spending five nights or an entire week in one spot isn't wrong; it's just more of a vacation than a trip. You'll have a smaller radius of deeper exploration.

Spending only one night in each place is doable but works only if the conditions are right. Those conditions are:

1. The area you're traveling in is small with tightly clustered attractions. You can see a lot without traveling far or staying long.
2. You have a rental car, or the country has a dependable transportation system, ensuring that your swift tempo won't hinder your chances of arriving and departing according to a preset plan.

When I traveled to the Balkans, I stayed in seven different cities in an eight-night span. If I could do it again, I would have moved slower, doubling up nights in larger cities and exploring smaller towns only by day. But the trip still worked because it was a road trip, and Croatia, Bosnia and Herzegovina, and Montenegro are compact and accessible.

Even after countless 9-Day Getaways, my wide-eyed appetite for adventure gets the best of me, and I travel too fast. When in doubt, slow down and spread out the itinerary.

SACRIFICIAL NIGHT

Sometimes you have to burn a night to make the rest of the itinerary work. This means staying somewhere less than ideal to avoid missing connections. It's the trip-planning equivalent of sacrificing your queen in a chess match. It may make you uneasy, but when executed at exactly the right moment, it's worth it.

Usually, a sacrificial night involves staying at an airport or port on the first or last night of a trip.

For example, when flying home to Seattle from Santorini via Frankfurt, the flight out of Santorini arrived in Frankfurt at midnight. We stayed at the airport Hilton, got cleaned up, slept a bit, and flew home the next morning.

On a family trip to French Polynesia, we stayed at an unimpressive hotel a few minutes away from the Papeete airport after a late-arriving long haul from LAX, before transferring to a luxury resort on Mo'orea the next morning.

When my Athens flights and Greek island ferries don't align, I'll occasionally stay overnight at a dingy hotel at the port.

Three pieces of advice for a sacrificial night:

1. Only do it if you must.
2. Write it into the itinerary, but treat it as a long layover.
3. When it's done, it's Voldemort: don't mention it.

ORDER UP

You know which places you want to stay and how long you want to stay in each of them. But how do you decide how to order them?

Usually, there's a logical geographic answer, a loop or coastal route with natural stopping points.

Sometimes it's not so obvious. Your targets may be scattered all over the map.

Especially in the latter case, it pays to consider the flow of the trip. Treat the trip as an album and each place you visit as a track on that album. The best albums are not only composed of excellent stand-alone tracks. They're deliberately arranged to create a harmonious whole. Your album should have an intro and outro, at least one radio hit, a backside that carries its weight, interludes, and possibly even skits.

A well-composed trip is balanced and cohesive. After blasting through a busy metropolis, opt for a quieter reprieve. Punctuate periods of potential monotony with spicy surprises.

THE HALFTIME SHOW

The middle of your trip is the best time to take a risk.

You could take an out-of-the-way day trip to a UNESCO site. For example, on Corfu, we decided to take a ferry to the mainland, then drive three hours inland to the monasteries of Meteora. The destination itself wasn't risky—I knew it would be stunning—but it would be a long day. I strategically positioned the adventure in the middle of my slow-paced, two-island Greece itinerary, knowing I'd have time to relax on the back half of my trip.

Annie and I enjoy staying at boutique design hotels. In the middle of our Australia trip, we left Byron Bay a day early and drove to Cabarita Beach to stay overnight at a hotel called Halcyon House. It was delightful, as we knew it would be. But the one-night stay sped up the pace of an already overcrowded trip. If we had stayed there earlier in the itinerary, we might have felt like we were missing some of Australia's bigger attractions. If we had stayed there near the end of the trip, the trip would have started to feel like an ice-cream sundae with too many toppings (yes, it's possible).

The last thing you want is to spend seven days of your trip recovering from a poorly executed, early gamble. And you certainly don't want to go home with a bad taste in your mouth from a wildcard detour that turned out to be a bit too wild.

SWEET HOME ALA-BOSNIA

"Where the hell am I right now?"

It's a question I've asked many times before on my travels, but this time, it rang especially loudly in my head.

My friend Jeremy and I started our nine-day jaunt across the Balkans in Split, Croatia. We spent two nights on the island of Brač before visiting Krka National Park. From there, most tourists would have traveled farther north, hugging the Adriatic coast and island-hopping all the way to Istria. We opted for Bosnia and Herzegovina.

Four hours after leaving Croatia, we arrived in Mostar, whose one famous attraction is its Ottoman-style bridge, which, along with most other historical sites in the city, was destroyed during the breakup of Yugoslavia and later rebuilt.

Croatia had been a vacation. Two days earlier, we had spent four hours eating chicken nuggets and drinking caipirinhas (better in Brazil) on Zlatni Rat, one of the most impressive beaches in the Adriatic. Mostar felt untamed in comparison.

Only a certain kind of traveler would have ventured there: one willing to sacrifice a night of their coastal summer holiday to take a chance on a wildcard destination where a common tourist pastime is searching for bullet holes.

We did what everyone does in Mostar: head straight for the bridge. Throughout the day, locals dive twenty-nine meters off the Stari Most (Old Bridge) into the Neretva River. After watching one man take the leap, I felt like I'd absorbed the essence of the place.

But the festivities were just heating up. A crowd was forming around an outdoor stage below the bridge, and we were the only tourists in it. A full choir of women in ballroom gowns belted out a Bosnian opera while a break-dancer wriggled on the stage in front of them. There was a DJ, band, and emcee/orchestrator who may also have been auctioneering. It was at once a concert, an award ceremony, an auction, a talent show, a dance competition, and a commencement.

This was Bosnia's best-case scenario, the essence of Otherwhere, a typical Tuesday for them, a martian encounter for us.

The event itself did not entertain us. It was the delightful randomness of stumbling upon it, like Alice into a tea party, that satisfied us to our curious cores. Mostar was an empty room lined with mystery doors; any we could have chosen led to revelry. We had nothing to fear, no expectations, no friends, no adversaries, and no desires.

Slipping out of the final, televised round of Bosnian Idol auditions, we moseyed away from the riverside and encountered quite a different, albeit equally festive, scene: a beer garden overflowing with expats and backpackers, featuring live bluegrass and classic rock.

I could have sworn I'd teleported when I heard "Sweet Home Alabama" reverberating out of an electric banjo. The motley crowd seemed like they'd been lounging there for centuries. We'd stumbled into the Bosnian Neverland and were drinking hefeweizens with the Lost Boys. None of them was a local; these were clearly foreigners, yet very much unlike us. They exuded an air of hippie nonchalance no mere passer-through could imitate. These were slow travelers. Regulars. They shared cups and knew the bartender's name.

I was already feeling blissfully displaced. Now I was so disoriented that I didn't know the difference between being lost and finding my way. We'd played the Mostar lottery and won, along with every other ticketholder. That's all it took to win the game of Bosnia and Herzegovina: throw away your preconceptions and play. It was a world so foreign to all who ventured through it that there could be no aliens. Everyone belonged.

So we did as the others and ate meat. Skewers. Kebabs. Lamb. Beef. Chicken and possibly rabbit. The restaurant was full to capacity except for one table in the back, closest to the wood-fired oven. The smoke was suffocating, the heat intense, but the platter they plopped on our table was positively voluminous. We scarfed our way to the bottom of it, revealing a pathetic patch of lettuce masquerading as a side salad and some chicken chunks pleading guilty to first-degree undercooked-ness. Our stomachs couldn't take any more pain. Drenched like we'd just leaped into the Neretva ourselves, we wondered how far into Montenegro our gastrointestinal misery would chase us.

It seemed only right to cap the night by sharing a hookah with a Dutch guy who lived in Switzerland and a Swiss guy who lived in Holland. Like everything else in Mostar, it was bewildering but not confusing; what you saw was what you got—a picturesque old bridge, a scarred place trying to heal, and two Americans trying not to puke.

I thought that maybe the next morning Mostar would explain itself, that the foreignness of the city would fade. That notion evaporated when we tried to pay for our hotel, which had assured us that they accepted credit cards. Nope. Cash only. We pulled out every last Croatian kuna and Bosnian mark we had, which happened to add up to exactly the cost of the room. How fitting to break even on Mostar, a place that offered only as much as we were willing to give it.

At the Montenegro border, we had to pay a toll but had no money left. The entire line of cars, which we spent two hours waiting in as the prior night's beef heap bubbled in our bellies, honked at us when we reached the kiosk to pay. We were, in that moment, the quintessential American jackasses. I remembered I had five US dollars in my backpack, dug for it, and pleaded with the border official to accept it. He performed a rough conversion in his head until he realized I had, technically, overpaid. Hating us and pocketing the five, he waved us out of B&H. Broke and hungry? More like bold and hopeful. That's a halftime show I'll never forget.

HIT THE HIGH NOTES

In the 1990s, psychologist Daniel Kahneman introduced the **peak-end rule,** which states that "people judge an experience largely based on how they felt at its peak (i.e., its most intense point) and at its end, rather than based on the total sum or average of every moment of the experience."

Applying peak-end theory to a trip itinerary means aiming for intensely pleasurable experiences along the way and making sure to go out with a bang. It's no surprise, then, that my favorite getaway ever was the one that ended on the highest note imaginable: my wedding.

Annie and I eloped in Santorini after spending three days each on Paros and Crete. There were no guests—just a wedding planner, photographer, and local Greek officiant (the only one on the island). The entire trip leading up to the intimate ceremony was our honeymoon, and the wedding itself was the dot of the exclamation mark of our Aegean escapade. Since we ended on such a high note, nothing that came before our grand finale in Santorini could tarnish our memory of that experience.

And just as the anticipation of a trip infuses the months before it with joy, our anticipation of tying the knot infused our days on Crete and Paros with the bliss of near matrimony. We cruised along the Libyan Sea and sipped freddo cappuccinos in the enchanting port of Naoussa, in disbelief that the best could still be yet to come. Every day, every moment felt like the trip's peak, and it was hard to fathom flying any higher.

By the time our officiant, who we hilariously saw marrying two other couples while we traipsed through Imerovigli for a photoshoot, now pronounced us husband [insert absurdly long, melodramatic pause here] and wife, we felt invincible.

If you intend to get married on your getaway, save it for last.

Roll Playback

Itinerary building is an exercise in seeing the future. When you think your itinerary is good enough, run through it from start to finish. Try your best to envision yourself in each moment of transition or uncertainty—disembarking a ten-hour flight, pulling up to the hotel, checking in and out, transferring ferries, catching a train, waiting in a taxi line, waking up in a foreign place.

How will you feel? Tired? Hungry? Scared? Eager? Energized? Will it matter? What will?

What can you do to ensure your needs are met?

What information do you still need to put your anxiety to rest?

Test the itinerary. Turn it upside down and shake it. What comes out? Gum wrappers and mushy bananas? Ideally, nothing.

Of course, at some point, you'll have to stop trying to make the itinerary perfect and call it good enough. With your nightly plan in place, your pace set, and your timepiece calibrated, you're ready for the slumber party.

CHAPTER 6

Shelter Out of Place

"There are no foreign lands. It is the
traveler only who is foreign."
—ROBERT LOUIS STEVENSON

I'VE SLEPT ON the mud floor of a Pondo hut on South Africa's
Wild Coast. I've shared a decrepit one-hundred-square-foot studio apartment in Recife, Brazil with two grown men. I've indulged
at the Amandari in Bali and crossed the Antarctic Circle in Cabin
212 on the stern of the *National Geographic Explorer*. I've experi-
mented with hostels, eco-lodges, bed and breakfasts, big resorts,
castles, and kibbutzim. If there's one thing I've learned from this
litany of lodgings, it's this: where you stay makes all the difference.

Staying Power

Sometimes a hotel is merely a bed. A single night at the Piraeus
Dream hotel, a dingy pitstop at the port of Athens, might amount
to no more than seven hours: a place to rest your head after a late

arrival before boarding an early ferry the next morning. (Somebody must have been rigging those Booking.com reviews—no chance in hell that place was a 9.2.)

But if you want it to be, a hotel can be a cultural gateway, a spiritual haven, or a culinary awakening. That was my experience at Miraval Wellness Resort in Arizona. The resort had it all: multiple dining options, pools, full-service spa, fitness center, tennis courts, programmed activities, and acres of desert terrain to explore by foot or on horseback.

There are myriad factors to consider when selecting accommodation. Here is a list of questions to help you clarify your values and intentions:

- **What purpose will it serve?** Are you looking for a place to crash or a home away from home?
- **What's your budget?** If all you need is a bed, the most affordable option is probably the right one. If you're more high maintenance or intend to spend a lot of time at your temporary abode, it's worth it to pay more for comfortable quarters.
- **Where is it located?** Is it in a certain area or neighborhood that's more convenient or alluring than others? Is it centrally located, two blocks from the train station, or accessible only via a winding dirt road?
- **What amenities must it offer?** Do you need laundry service? A kitchenette? Parking spot? Proper gym to get your morning workout in? Is fast and free internet all that matters? You can never go wrong with air-conditioning.
- **What's your ideal atmosphere?** Are you looking for a lively social scene or trying to avoid one? A romantic place with no kids allowed? Something serene? Cozy? Upbeat?

Understated? Smaller hotels are more intimate. Bigger hotels are more businesslike. Boutique hotels (my preference) win at style.

- **What room features do you require?** How much space do you need to be comfortable? A small room with private outdoor space could feel palatial. What about a desk? Mini fridge? Pull-out couch? About that air-conditioning...

Every aspect of your lodging can cater to your preferences. If you're easy to please, find a conveniently located, affordable option that gets good ratings on reputable sites. If you're choosy, dial in your nonnegotiables and don't compromise. A nonsmoker in a smoking room doesn't care how comfy the mattress is.

BOOKENDS

The first and last nights of your getaway are the bookends that hold it all together. You'll likely be exhausted and disoriented when you hit the ground in a new country. A modern hotel is your best option.

A larger, chain hotel can be ideal for the final night of your trip when you'll want a dependable place to get cleaned up before heading home. For example, after my sister and I stayed at Gyoku-zoin, a Buddhist temple near Nara, the Shinjuku Hilton eased our transition back into urban life.

The bookend hotel on your last night can help to ensure a smooth return voyage. Get some exercise and a respectable breakfast. Avoid scavenging for an oat milk latte on the streets of Santiago when your flight to Miami is already boarding at Gate C5.

MIX IT UP

Diversifying your accommodation is a way to hedge your bets so that one bad pick won't sink your whole itinerary. Mixing and matching different hotel flavors also maximizes your getaway's story-yielding potential.

It pays to seek out unusual accommodation on at least one night of your trip—a Rinzai monastery, shared chalet, or holistic healing hideaway. These interludes add intrigue to the itinerary. They're the jokers in the deck. You'll remember your wildcards much longer than you'll pine for the Marriott's breakfast buffet.

Likewise, it can be beneficial to vary your types of stays in strategic order. The accommodation you choose on a given night should take into consideration where you'll be coming from and where you're going next. For example, after spending a night at a tent camp in the Dubai desert, I reeked of smoke and had sand spilling out of my hair. Returning to the city, I checked straight into a luxury hotel to freshen up before catching a flight to Muscat, Oman.

Get a Room

It's movie night, and you need something to watch. The browsing begins. Many a trailer is viewed. Two hours, twelve previews, and three false starts later, you're exhausted and go to bed.

Booking hotels can be just as wearisome as picking flicks. But it doesn't have to be.

SEEK REFUGE

Aggregators like TripAdvisor and Kayak skim the internet's hotel foam, and Google now lists both hotels and vacation rentals at google.com/travel/hotels. But the irresistibly easy-to-use OTA Booking.com is my go-to site for hotel search. You'll enjoy it as long as you can look past the egregious scarcity marketing ("Hurry! Only 1 Room Left!").

Despite my professed detestation of OTAs for flight-searching, I still recommend Booking.com for browsing hotels. It almost always lists a free cancellation option that isn't available or may be buried on the hotel's site. It's also convenient for stringing together a nightly itinerary and seeing all of your reservations in one place.

Singular boutique hotels are harder to find, as they should be. I start my search at **Mr. and Mrs. Smith,** a tasteful curator of independent hotels. As a Hyatt loyalist, I always peruse offerings on **Small Luxury Hotels of the World,** one of Hyatt's strategic partners. The SLH portfolio is jaw-dropping. If *Condé Nast Traveler* or *Departures* touts the property I'm considering, all the better.

RESERVE YOUR SPOT

Although browsing hotels is breezy on Booking.com, I like supporting hotels, especially smaller ones, by booking directly with them (if the price and terms are the same or better).

To fight back against the dominion of OTAs, many hotels offer discounts to incentivize direct bookings. If the OTA listing is cheaper, it may be a binding reservation.

Loyalty is another reason to book direct. Members of hotel rewards programs may qualify for discounted rates and additional perks. Booking directly with hotels can also yield superior customer service. It's easier to reserve specific rooms and make special requests, like a six-pack of chocolate stout, a pair of ankle weights, or a monogrammed pool noodle.

Above all, booking direct protects you against the hassle of trying to get help from a real person if your plans go awry. No disappearing reservations or hours spent on hold in the 1-800 vortex.

Like booking flights, booking lodging requires extra deliberation at checkout. When you're overly eager to pony up, you're also most likely to botch your arrival and departure dates, miss hidden fees, pay in the wrong currency, and reserve an oceanfront suite with a panoramic parking lot view. You've come too far and played too well to choke in the fourth quarter.

CANCEL CULTURE

I had two trips planned for April and June 2020, both of which I had to cancel due to COVID. I'm pleased to say I got refunds for every hotel and flight from both trips (although it took four months and formal disputes to Chase and Amex). Regardless of COVID, I was entitled to the refunds because I had paid extra for free cancellation.

Post-pandemic, I'll think long and hard before booking a hotel without the option to cancel with no penalty, even if I have to pay more for that option. The peace of mind you get from a flexible hotel booking is priceless.

Don't be lackadaisical in the planning process, knowing you can bail on the plan at any time. Even if you do pay extra for the right to cancel with no penalty, canceling can still be a burden. You may need to wait weeks for the hotel to refund your deposit.

If you're so confident in the immutability of your itinerary and so enamored by the price of a hotel without free cancellation, go ahead and save the money. But err on the side of caution when you do.

When I booked a three-night stay at a boutique hotel on the Cycladic island of Sifnos, I paid extra for free cancellation, not because I sensed a pandemic brewing but because the stay hinged on a ferry schedule that hadn't been released yet. It was a small, in-demand hotel at the beginning of the season, and I knew it would fill up if I waited. When I booked it, I remember thinking, *If I had that schedule, I could save $200!* In light of COVID, I ultimately saved much more than that.

On the same canceled trip to the Cyclades, I'd made another reservation at an Airbnb. Securing the refund was particularly challenging. The reservation fell just outside of Airbnb's extenuating circumstances policy, which guaranteed refunds for bookings through June 15, 2020. I missed the cutoff by five days. I had to request a letter from United Airlines proving that they had terminated my flights and I had not voluntarily canceled. Thankfully, Airbnb granted an exception and gave me a refund.

I got lucky. Cancellation policies on short-term rental sites like Airbnb and VRBO are fickle. Horrendous disputes between renters and property managers abound.

Whether you choose Airbnb, some other vacation rental service, or opt for a hotel, examine the cancellation policy and avoid overly rigid ones. You endured 2020, so it shouldn't be too hard to take worst-case scenarios into consideration.

HAPPY AS CAN B&B

I recommend Airbnb over hotels when you're traveling in a group, when hotels are limited, or if you have a fantasy about living like a local in a certain place.

When I booked a solo sojourn to Havana in 2015, all of the guesthouses I was interested in were fully booked. I turned to Airbnb and found a centrally located apartment in Old Havana.

Passing through Barcelona for a conference in Costa Brava, I scored a trendy one-bedroom flat in the Gràcia neighborhood. I wasn't planning on spending much time inside and was willing to forgo a hotel breakfast to feel like a young Picasso.

When it comes to cleanliness, the Airbnb versus hotel debate rages on. Although every competent hotel has implemented rigorous cleaning protocols, highly trafficked lobbies and common areas pose additional risk. Airbnbs require less in-person interaction, but if a host has ever ghosted you when you pulled up to the apartment and asked for the code to the key box, a proper check-in is probably the least of your concerns. Look for the Enhanced Clean badge on Airbnb listings if you're the kind of person who won't sneeze unless the CDC approves it first.

Vacation rentals may be pricier and harder to book than hotels, but their potential upside is enormous. A summer cottage or villa in Europe will require a reservation far in advance. These rentals typically have longer minimum stays (often one week, Sunday to Sunday) and are therefore trickier to claim and cancel. However, if you want privacy and slow immersion, there is no better choice.

NO KOALA FOR YOU

We had reservations at a quiet bed and breakfast perched on a hill with an ocean view (the ocean kind, not the parking lot kind) and a koala (supposedly) in the tree above our balcony.

When we got to the accommodation, the hosts weren't there. They left us a key. It was 110°F in the room and 95°F outside, so opening the patio door did little to cool it down. The fan was broken. The bed was stiff. There was no AC. And there was no koala.

The only thing the room had going for it was the view, but we didn't need the view to fall asleep. So we did what any unapologetic, uncompromising guests (who had already paid) would do. We said, "Eff it" and drove three hours back to Melbourne.

Yup. We threw in the Great Ocean Towel. Winding our way east, we booked an impromptu room at a contemporary hotel called Ovolo Laneways in the CBD.

SHELTER OUT OF PLACE

Hauling back to Melbourne was arguably the best part of the whole road trip because it felt so good to say, "Change of plans. We're leaving," rather than force ourselves to stay somewhere we'd selected online that failed us in reality.

The accommodation you select should enable and enhance your getaway. If there's no air-conditioning and squinting at a eucalyptus tree for twenty minutes doesn't conjure any koalas, call a different play and find somewhere that aligns with your mood and mission statement.

No matter where you stay, you're bound to bump into surprises. Some may be breezy; others may be sweltering. Be bold and realistic in your selection process. Take a chance on immersive or unusual lodging. Select and order your sleepovers strategically across your itinerary. Strike a balance between safe bets and eclectic dwellings. Book them with confidence and, whenever possible, with flexible policies. If the plan sucks, change it. Twist with the plot. Sleep well.

Roger that? Let's get moving.

CHAPTER 7

Be Transported

"When dealing with complex transportation issues,
the best thing to do is pull up with a cold beer and let
somebody else figure it out."
—ANTHONY BOURDAIN

ACCORDING TO GOOGLE Maps, we would arrive at the port of Igoumenitsa two minutes before the ferry departed. If we missed it, we'd have to wait for two hours to catch the last crossing at 9:30 p.m., which would put us back in Corfu Town at 11:00 p.m., and back at our villa around midnight. The day trip from northeast Corfu to the monasteries of Meteora was ambitious enough without added delays. If we missed the early ferry, our memorable excursion would devolve into an exhausting circus.

Annie pushed our dinky diesel rental car to the brink, eking out every extra kilometer per hour she could. I tried to buy tickets from my phone, hoping to shave precious minutes by paying in advance. No luck. Greek ferries leave either exactly on time or four hours late, so I knew we had to beat the clock. Annie was gaining back minutes. We still had a chance.

We pulled into the port with seconds to spare. I jumped out of our valiant Peugeot and barged up to the Blue Star Ferries counter amid a crowd of Greeks vying for the last remaining space.

I have witnessed the loading and unloading of countless ferries across the Aegean. I've seen seven rolling suitcases strapped to a single donkey. I've coughed clouds of cigarette smoke in the Athens airport taxi line. The Greeks are port people. They've mastered the art of loading and unloading, making it fit, and insisting they've got it under control. Our boat hadn't left, and we had a tiny car, which is how I knew we were getting on. But not by being polite.

I waved a wad of cash at the Blue Star ticket woman. She snatched it and replaced it with my ticket and change using only one hand.

Feeling victorious, I motioned at Annie to abandon all etiquette, veer through the cluster of idling cars, and drive aboard. Having the ticket meant the fare was paid, not that our place on that ship was promised. The affronted ferry traffic controller commanded her to halt. We both held our breath, waiting to see if our efforts had been heroic or futile. He loaded a slew of semis onto the ship, and as we watched each one drive aboard, the agony of deciphering what it meant for us became unbearable. Had he told us his final no, or were we waiting our turn?

Reluctantly, he checked our ticket and, as the crowd that only we could hear cheered, he waved us on. We pulled within millimeters of the car ahead. Seconds later, they lifted the ramp. I thought it might crush our bumper.

Sure, we could have been more cordial about boarding the ferry. But pulling up with a cold beer and letting someone else figure it out works a lot better when you're traveling with your own film crew. When dealing with complex transportation issues, it's best to be assertive but not aggressive and take a stand without making a scene.

Sadly, foreign countries do not rearrange themselves to satisfy your every whim. You must be unabashed about asking for, and sometimes demanding, what you want. If your hotel room smells like diapers, switch rooms. If your tour guide tries to convince you Old Dubai is historically relevant even though it contains a Seattle's Best Coffee and that Bedouin snake charmer is a paid actor, walk away. And if there's no more space on the car ferry to Corfu, make them make space.

The Strongest Link

Linking transportation—how you get between cities—may include short flights, long bus or car rides, trains, ferries, or dragons.

For most destinations, you can get away with planning linking transportation after you've solidified your nightly plan. If you know you'll be able to get between cities or towns any day you want (if, for example, you'll have a car or access to a train that runs constantly), there's no downside to booking an accommodation before you connect the dots.

When linking transportation options are sporadic, lock yours down before selecting nightly stops. There's no point in booking a hotel somewhere unless you're positive you can get there and that it will be worth the effort.

A missed ferry in Greece could seriously disrupt the flow of a trip. You might not see another one for days. Same goes for flights on Uzbekistan Airways that leave on Tuesdays and Fridays in spring, Mondays and Saturdays in summer, and take lengthy

lunch breaks at Qdoba without even texting to say they're running late.

Every itinerary has a weak link or pressure point on which all
other legs of the trip depend. The more likely a missed connection
is to set off a chain reaction, the more priority it deserves in your
planning hierarchy.

POINT A TO POINT G

You may not have a choice in your mode of transportation. Getting from Chiang Mai to Luang Prabang, a bus may be your only
option.

When you do have a choice, your priorities, as always, are paramount. Which of the following factors are most important to you?

- **Speed and convenience.** You want to get from Ankara to
  Tbilisi as simply and directly as possible.
- **Timeliness and reliability.** You need something you can
  count on because if you miss this train to Berlin, you'll be
  stuck in Bruges for another night, and you're all set with
  Bruges.
- **Comfort and cleanliness.** The sheets in your Soviet-era
  sleeper wagon on the Turkestan-Siberia railway haven't
  been washed in forty-six years, and you don't feel great
  about it.
- **Safety.** You wouldn't traverse the "Road of Death" from La
  Paz to Yungas if someone paid you a million bolivianos.
- **Affordability.** You're willing to compromise on speed and
  comfort to save some cheddar.
- **Scenery.** You're willing to compromise on speed and com-
  fort to see beautiful sights and sigh longingly.

Whether your mode of transport is a train, car, bus, or hovercraft, it can't let you down if you choose it deliberately, recognizing its advantages and potential pitfalls.

The **Rome2rio** app shows you all of your transportation options from point A to point B (or F, or G), mapping plausible routes and taking the dread out of navigation logistics. Countries and cities normally have their own rail and bus sites or apps to facilitate browsing schedules and purchasing tickets. A guidebook can also come in handy to steer you toward a trusted vendor.

Book in advance to avoid high-stress signage deciphering and currency calculations in hectic stations.

STRIKING DISTANCES

In the planning phase, travelers often underestimate durations. They spend their entire trip getting from one destination to the next, leaving no time to be anywhere.

Say you take four short flights instead of two long train rides. You're still going to have to cross four security checkpoints and get yourself to and from the airport eight times. That's not necessarily more efficient.

Airport, train, bus, and ferry connection times tend to look more innocuous than they are. Forty-five minutes in the Frankfurt international terminal? You'll barely make it through the duty-free store.

Distances can be especially deceptive. Planning a 9-Day Getaway to Colombia with my friend Josh, I felt confident we could tag the coffee triangle and Caribbean coast with an inflatable canoe and two scooters. Then Josh sent me a map of the country with the state of Washington overlaid on top of it (from thetruesize.com). Apparently, Colombia is six times as big as my home state. We chose to fly from Bogotá to Cartagena and save the electric trikes for a smaller country. I'm thinking Qatar.

Round up on minutes and mileage. Assume there will be delays. Make your itinerary wait for you. Don't chase it.

Renting a Car

The collision damage waiver they try to upsell you. The infinitesimal windshield crack they claim was your fault. The sedan that reeks of cigarettes and looks nothing like the one you reserved...

I love driving in foreign countries and recommend it for exploring swaths of scenic terrain in a short span of time or to access otherwise inaccessible locales. But why does renting a car abroad always feel like such a boondoggle? Allow me to pulverize the pain points.

UNDERCOVERAGE

It happens at every car rental counter across the globe. A scare tactic to prey on timid, uninformed drivers. The dreaded collision damage waiver sales pitch. Ugh.

It sounds so simple: buy a waiver to cover the cost of the vehicle in case of damage. But the agent's slimy insistence sounds your internal alarm. What's the catch?

Cost, for starters. A CDW could run you up to 50 percent of the daily rental rate. Even if you're willing to pay for it, you may still want to decline the offer.

Your personal auto insurance likely won't cover you abroad, but your credit card might. Always call your credit card providers to get clear about what coverage, if any, you already have. Find out if your card provides primary coverage or secondary coverage. Primary coverage kicks in first, overriding your personal policy. This saves you from filing a claim. If you don't have an existing auto insurance policy, your credit card's secondary coverage becomes primary.

Ask about exceptions for specific countries or vehicle types (no promises for a Jeep Wrangler in Costa Rica). When you've chosen your prize-winning plastic, slap that bad boy on the rental counter like you're flipping over pocket aces.

Friendly reminder: owning a credit card with collision protection doesn't entitle you to those benefits unless you pay with it.

Never agree to the CDW the agent pushes unless you're positive you won't have any protection without it.

THAT'S THE TICKET

Driving in Australia, I stopped at a red light on a one-way street, then turned left onto another one-way street. I figured it worked just like making a right turn in the States. I was immediately pulled over, surrounded by four cops and forced to take a Breathalyzer. They descended on me like vultures! Let off with a warning, I drove away like a limping kangaroo, carefully remembering to signal. I flipped the windshield wipers instead.

Italy got me, too. A month after I returned from the boot, Avis courteously forwarded me a $350 citation from the Italian government. A stationary camera had nabbed me illegally driving through a construction zone in Rome as I followed my GPS's instructions onto the SS7 highway to Amalfi. I recall neither the violation nor any malicious intent but promptly paid the fine when I noticed a warning that failing to do so would result in my permanent banishment from the country. No chance. I'm just getting started with those tomatoes.

Wonky rules. Foreign signage. Carefree exuberance. It's a delicate combination. If you plan to drive internationally, learn the rules of the road. Assume you're being watched at all times. Avoid construction zones and never turn on red. But no matter how many times you get lost, fined, chided, or admonished, enjoy yourself. That's the ticket.

ON LOCATION

I recommend GPS when you rent a car, but the agency's navigation system should be your last resort. Instead, download Google Maps for offline use. Newer cars with built-in navigation systems could save you the hassle of setting up a portable device and may be preferable to downloaded maps on your phone, propped up in the cupholder (BYO suction windshield mount?). Some travelers swear by their Garmin or TomTom GPS devices. If I were going to buy a single-purpose electronic device, I'd much rather have a Walkman, PalmPilot, or Game Boy.

GONNA NEED TO SEE SOME ID

I've rented cars on five continents and have never needed an International Driver's permit. I have been asked for it, though. My US driver's license always suffices. I imagine it would be a slight inconvenience to get pulled over in some small village in Hungary with only a Washington State driver's license, but that would still make a better story than visiting my local AAA office and paying $20 for an International Driver's permit I'll never use.

OLD CAR SMELL

Even worse than the stench of mildew is the musk of having been misled. Here are a few more rental tips to avoid the odor of defeat:

- If possible, utilize a "pick from the row" option to choose the exact car you want in person.

- Inspect the car before you pull away—as thoroughly as you would if it were brand new. Any scuff, scratch, or stain that goes unnoted can and will be used against you.
- Don't assume they'll have automatic transmission cars available. If you can't drive stick, expect to pay more, and for the rental car agent to judge you for not knowing how to drive a car.
- Factor in fuel costs. Gas can be expensive, especially in Iceland, Albania, and the Central African Republic.
- Be careful with pickup and drop-off times. They're often in twenty-four-hour increments, and an extra hour could translate to an extra day on your invoice.

ROLL WITH IT

We picked up our Renault Captur at Split Airport and cruised away into Dalmatia.

The car was good enough to be our trusted chariot across the Balkans. Yes, it was the cheapest car that Sixt Rental Cars offered, and yes, for twenty bucks more per day we could have rented a BMW instead. But all we really needed was an automatic with air-conditioning. The Captur fit the bill.

Unfortunately, it also had a nail in its back left tire. The hazard light didn't come on right away. It waited until we hit the highway the next morning, just as the boundlessly optimistic, first-full-day-of-the-trip, anything-is-possible feeling set in.

We headed straight back to Split Airport to swap vehicles.

I liked our new Fiat 500. The AC was stronger and the interior sleeker, although the center console was about as wide as an armrest in coach. Great tire pressure, though.

We made it three-quarters of the way to Krka National Park before the Fiat stopped accelerating. It maxed out at 70 kph. Our comrades at the Sixt airport kiosk promised they'd help us sort it out.

We idled into the Krka parking lot after getting passed, honked, and glared at by no fewer than seventy-four other drivers, and explored the park while Sixt brought us yet another replacement car. When we returned to the lot, a sparkling BMW 1-Series hatchback, mounted on a tow truck, awaited.

We inspected the BMW like a judge at the Westminster Kennel Club Dog Show inspecting a bichon frise. It won Best in Show.

It is entirely plausible that for some other bargain-hunting tourists, the Renault Captur at Sixt in Split steers toward a problem-free road trip, devoid of hazard lights and tow trucks. I'm sure the cheapest option works out splendidly for many people in many situations. But in our particular case, the irony of finally ending up with the "expensive" BMW that we had originally considered and passed on was not lost on me.

I won't necessarily rent a Beemer next time I need a car, but whatever whip I choose, I'll roll with it—even if it doesn't roll with me.

Along for the Ride

Getting between cities is the biggest piece of the transportation equation. But don't forget the small, easily neglected transportation assists you may need—airport shuttles, private cars, local bus rides, taxi rides, chopper flights, and camel caravans. Book these localized transportation legs after your intercity links. They're advisable but not essential to arrange in advance.

But if you've made it this far, you might as well go all the way. After you hone your daily plans, fill in the gaps to ensure you'll move smoothly from one attraction to the next. Maybe you can walk. Maybe you can Uber. Day pass on the metro? Flag a rickshaw?

Don't be intimidated by public transportation. It can be a breeze. If it's not, at least you'll learn how the locals get around.

Ask your hotel for help arranging excursions. When Annie and I visited Mexico City, Hotel Condesa DF secured us a driver to Teotihuacán and a private tour of the pyramids. There were no surprises or price negotiations, which made the huevos rancheros I ate in the hotel courtyard that morning taste even better.

Driving, cycling, flying, ferrying, scooting, ballooning, hitching, or skipping through a foreign country should be fun. Solving train riddles, decoding maps, and sticking it to slimy car rental agents epitomizes mindful travel. To jostle onto jam-packed ships and avoid arrest for pathfinding peccadilloes—this is what you came for.

Now put the Peugeot in park and let's go exploring.

CHAPTER 8

Food, Fun, Freedom

"To move, to breathe, to fly, to float,
To gain all while you give,
To roam the roads of lands remote,
To travel is to live."

—HANS CHRISTIAN ANDERSEN

WANDERING THROUGH A market in Mumbai in the late evening, I entered a shoe shop and found a pair I liked. Traditional woven moccasins with square toes, thatched with three different hues of leather.

I appreciated them for the intricate craftsmanship that went into making them. Maybe I'd don them on a balmy night in Palm Springs.

So I tried them on. The shop attendant offered me a shoehorn and smiled. It felt so familiar to the times I'd purchased shoes at Nordstrom in downtown Seattle. All that was missing from the successful transaction was the silver shopping bag.

The next day, I resolved to make the slippers a summer fashion staple. There was only one problem: they were too big. I needed to go back to the shop to exchange them. *I'll go a half size down. I'll bring the receipt. Nordstrom has exceptional customer service.*

Passing the market on the way to dinner, I instructed my taxi driver to stop and wait as I ran back to swap my slippers for a snugger pair. Crossing the street at rush hour and not dying was a small miracle. The market was packed.

I dodged my way to the stall. It had shrunk to the size of an airplane galley. Where before there had been two people—me and the shop owner—there were now easily forty.

There I was speaking fluent Touristese, dangling my barely too-big traditional Indian moccasins, trying to get somebody's attention. A shop attendant inspected my return merchandise and seemed to understand exactly what I wanted. He grabbed the shoes from my hand, threw them like plum pits to the back of the shop, snatched a completely different kind of shoe off the wall in a size that would have been big on Shaq, dipped his bare hand in a bucket of lacquer, smeared it all over the replacement shoes, shoved them in a plastic bag that reeked of saffron and cow, and pushed me out of the store.

Only three mopeds grazed me on the steeplechase back to my taxi with a sopping sack of souvenir in hand.

Find Dining

I have no recollection of dinner that night in Mumbai. The shoe shop stole the show. With or without a pre-prandial detour, deliberate travelers have plenty of options to discover and share memorable meals abroad.

TripAdvisor is decent, but the reviews are hard to trust and tedious to sift through. **TimeOut** and **Eater** are useful research tools for finding culinary hotspots. **Instagram** is another useful way to discover new restaurants; search for a city or neighborhood and note the restaurants geotagged on the most mouth-watering posts. Save contenders in Google Maps.

The way to find the best food is to ask locals or, even better, eat with them. Meal-sharing apps are on the rise, making social eating, in-home cooking lessons, and culinary experiences easily available. **EatWith** brings people together with food in over 130 countries. **Traveling Spoon** connects travelers with vetted locals for home-cooked gastronomic delights. **Cesarine** promises the best culinary experiences in Italy. **Airbnb** is also doing its best to make dinner in a foreign country a cross-cultural learning opportunity.

Vegans, vegetarians, and healthy food snobs (guilty) will rejoice in an app called **HappyCow**, which can be a lifesaver in a city that claims pig's knee among its delicacies (I'm looking at you, Prague).

Adventurous eaters should always try the local specialty. Seek out the best iteration of the most beloved dish in any location: goulash, tagine, vindaloo, plov, or pizza. Picky eaters should prepare to have eyes rolled at them when they ask for what they want—and ask anyway.

You may want a restaurant in the center of the action, but the better and better-priced meal may be around the corner. When you find a winning restaurant, follow the streusel crumbs to the next exceptional eatery. Where else does the chef recommend?

Make reservations and always try to find multiple dining options in case one falls through. Try to pick specific lunch and dinner spots for each day of your trip so you always know where your next meal will be. If you can't zero in on exact restaurants, at least target a specific street or cluster of restaurants. Hangry desperation ruins trips and relationships (or so I've heard). Step your snack game up just in case.

Finally, spend a few minutes researching the dining etiquette at your destination. In Georgia, only sip your wine during a toast. In Jordan, shake your coffee cup to avoid an unwanted refill.

Wherever you get away, eat well.

Tours de Force

The cruise docked in Ocho Rios, Jamaica. Passengers had paid hundreds of dollars in advance for prearranged tours—an excursion to Dunn's River Falls, a rainforest adventure to mystic mountain, or a visit to Bob Marley's mausoleum.

I couldn't figure out what everyone was paying for. If I wanted to visit a waterfall, why couldn't I just catch a taxi to take me there and jump in? What were the tours providing that I couldn't arrange myself?

The tradeoff between self-directed exploration and prepackaged excursions is a microcosm of the decision to plan your own getaway or hire a travel agency to build your trip for you. At least look into how you would arrange a day tour independently before you sign up for a guided tour. You can probably save time and money by piecing it together on your own.

If you do opt for a guided tour, join the smallest possible group. Try a private or small-group tour from **Context Travel** with experts in their fields or a cultural tour with **Tastemakers Africa**.

Only do day tours that provide a dangerous, gear-intensive, or one-of-a-kind experience you couldn't safely replicate on your own, like beekeeping in the English countryside, paragliding in the Julian Alps, or snorkeling with whale sharks in Mozambique.

Use day tours as excuses to put yourself in the uncomfortable role of a novice. If you're just paying for someone to hold your hand while you do something you already know how to do in a slightly more challenging context, don't bother.

In remote destinations or on trips with many moving parts, a full-time, private guide can take all the hassle out of getting around. My trusted guide in Uzbekistan, Zahid, added so much value to my trip that I couldn't believe I almost toured the country without him. He translated, negotiated, arranged transport, and finessed access to otherwise off-limits attractions (no one had climbed the Kalon minaret in Bukhara in at least five years). By the end of the trip, we had become close friends.

Private guides provide more than knowledge; they ensure the trip is painless and efficient. Hire a reputable agency and communicate your priorities clearly. You'll likely be able to explore more, with less stress, than you would on your own.

Quick Questing

A translator would have been helpful when I was buying my wedding ring in Tokyo.

I'd decided on a Japanese style called *mokumegane*, which fuses different precious metals into a woodgrain pattern. I'd researched the jewelers in Tokyo who specialized in this style and had a list of three stores on which my hopes rested.

I was traveling with my sister, whose style advice I've been depending on since adolescence, and we were at the source. So the odds were in my favor, I thought.

The first store was closed. The second store didn't exist. But the third store was open, and it was perfect.

We drank tea as they brought out boxes of rings in various sizes and finishes. I wasn't the first English speaker they'd served. They offered me a laminated binder of survey questions about my preferences. One page had a friendly reminder about fluctuating finger sizes followed by the delightfully translated phrase: "Please do not too much nervous." Tell me that's not the best travel (and life) mantra of all time.

The ring quest was a success in every way. It gave me and my sister a chance to experience impeccable Japanese customer service and attention to detail up close. It led to deeper conversations about marriage and life plans. And I got a custom *mokumegane* ring from Ginza that makes me happy every time I look at it.

In the process, we also explored three different neighborhoods in Tokyo. Leaving the ring store, we stumbled upon one of the best tempura restaurants in the city, which made headlines for denying Barack Obama a seat when he showed up to the full restaurant with no reservation. Two people had canceled at the last minute. We waltzed up to the counter to enjoy an impromptu Michelin star lunch.

Even if your trip is not an epic hero's journey, you can still reap the benefits of a goal-driven journey with the aid of miniature quests. A mini quest is a stand-alone mission or subgoal of the trip's larger focus. Your quest might be as simple as finding a pair of tea towels to add to your collection, as frivolous as finding a sun hat to wear for the rest of your trip, or as contemplative as finding the perfect vantage point to sketch. It can be the difference between a day spent aimlessly wandering around a new city (which isn't necessarily bad) and a day imbued with a sense of initiative and achievement.

BE CAREFUL WHAT YOU WAIT FOR

On Rue des Rosiers in Paris, the line for King Falafel Palace was thirty meters long. It smelled good, it looked good, and it was clearly the spot for falafel. With a line that long, it had to be the real deal.

Directly across the street from King Falafel Palace, there was another falafel joint. The spinning shawarma looked just as juicy. The veggies looked fresh. The counter was clean. And there was no line—not a single customer.

I felt bad for the restaurant with no business but figured there must be a good reason for the discrepancy in patronage. I didn't come all the way to Paris to eat the second-best falafel in Le Marais, so I waited in the long line like everybody else.

The King's falafel was hands-down the best I've ever had, but I still can't say for sure that it was worth the wait. Who knows, the hapless reject's pitas could have been even better. Next time I'm in Paris, I'll find out.

Lines are social proof that a certain spot is worth the wait. When your time is limited, it's your responsibility to gauge whether the socially trending tzatziki sauce is really worth it.

Most attractions have some variation of a fast pass for which you can pay extra to skip the line. Always find out in advance if such an option exists.

La Galleria dell'Accademia in Florence has a skip-the-line option for advanced reservations. When I first visited, I showed up without a reservation and decided to queue for two hours to see Michelangelo's marvelous *David*. It was worth the wait, although many tourists are willing to settle for the *David* replica in Piazza della Signoria (it's not the same).

People have waited in much longer lines for much less impressive attractions. The only wrong way to wait is to not anticipate that you might have to.

Museum Peace

The irregular ambling. The posing and pondering. The stops and starts, deceptive distances, and inspiration overload. Museum fatigue is real. I leave all the best museums feeling like I have no knees and no brain.

You have to really want the experience. If you do, prepare for it. Research the exhibits in advance and decide which ones are most appealing. Just as you're not under any contractual obligation to finish every book you start (except this one), you're under no obligation to see every exhibit a museum contains. Move at your own speed. Blast through like you're on a scavenger hunt or sit and stare until you melt into the wall. Consider setting a time limit so you don't feel confined and forget where you are.

Musée Picasso in Antibes is one of my favorite museums because the museum itself is a work of art. Its windows frame the Mediterranean so it, too, is on display. A stunning terrace makes the sea feel as accessible as the sculptures that adorn it. Seek out museums like this, which blend into their surroundings, offer outdoor spaces, or otherwise deviate from the maze-like paradigm.

Going to a museum should never feel like going to IKEA. But given the high likelihood that you'll be exhausted after you visit one, plan a meal or chill post-visit activity to recompose yourself and reflect on the marvels you witnessed.

Free Lunch

Peppering your travel days with tours and reservations can backfire if you're not careful. Nonstop appointments might make you feel trapped, not free.

FOOD, FUN, FREEDOM

For travelers concerned about planning themselves into a more rigid schedule than the one they were trying to get away from, designated free time is the answer.

If you want to wander aimlessly, leaving your discoveries up to serendipity, carve out time to do it. Getting lost is a lot more enjoyable when you do it on purpose.

If you need it, give yourself the time and permission to do nothing. And if your only plan is to abandon all plans, at least make a contingency plan in case you grow bored or restless. This could be as simple as identifying one site, hike, or café. When it comes to following your dreams in life, "Forget plan B" is excellent advice. For travel dreams, not so much.

Remember plan B, and consider plan C, too. Always keep your eye on the nearest exit, especially if there's a reasonable probability that you'll need to use it. What if the sole café in the tiny village you're heading to for lunch is closed? What if the line for the shrine goes around the block?

If odds are that you won't be able to run the play you called, have a new play ready. That way, even your nothing will be something.

Happy Accidents

My Mumbai moccasins never fully dried, and their stench never fully faded. I lament to inform you that I got rid of them. When I bade them farewell, I realized that it wasn't the shoes themselves I prized. It was the absurd mocs-in-translation situation.

There's a place and time for spontaneous detours and flagrant falafel lines. Those happy accidents may turn out to be your trip's Cinderella slipper. Reserving tables and tours to anchor your itinerary makes the shoes fit. Your meals and activities should be their

127

own miniature getaways, approached with the same harmonious blend of intention and insouciance you bring to the trip as a whole.

The most hackneyed travel quote of all time, from J. R. R. Tolkien, is true: "Not all those who wander are lost." Most of those who wander, however, are extremely lost. A lost wanderer pays Princess Cruises $175 to drive them to a waterfall. A not-lost wanderer has a backup plan and would never settle for a disproportional David.

The meals and fun you weave into your trip design should serve as signposts to ensure you never completely lose your way. You can erase or ignore them as easily as you drew them up. You make the rules. You choose where to wait and when to leave. That's freedom worth paying for. Keep the receipt.

CHAPTER 9

Pre-Departure Peace of Mind

"If you really want to escape the things that harass you, what you're needing is not to be in a different place but to be a different person."

—SENECA

THE NIGHT BEFORE our wedding trip to Greece, my emotionally stable wife, who rarely cries, burst into tears.

I was so confused. We had been planning for four months. The whole trip was dialed in. There was nothing to be anxious about.

She wasn't anxious about going to Greece or being there. She was anxious about returning to disorder. Touché.

Preparing to leave for a trip means preparing to return from it. Pre-departure days can be overwhelming, but would you rather be stressed out the night before your trip or the entire time you're on it?

If you do your pre-departure homework, you won't be stressed at all.

For All You Care

When my parents used to make me clean my room, I did what any shrewd teenage slob would do: shoved all my crap in the closet. See? My room's not messy anymore.

That hack was hardly sustainable. Travelers who shirk their pre-trip responsibilities are going to have a very hard time getting dressed for school tomorrow.

Shortcuts are especially tempting as the main event nears. But the travel preparation that seems most unrelated to your getaway can be among the most essential to ensure its seamless execution. Neglect these tasks at your own peril.

HOME CARE

Before you vacate the premises, it's your duty to whip your space into shape. Returning to a clean and orderly home is restorative in its own way. Nothing screams order like a bulleted list:

- Clean your home thoroughly or hire cleaners to come a day or two before you leave. If you have regular housekeepers you trust, you might even have them come while you're away.
- Put a set of clean sheets on your bed.
- Empty all trash bins, especially the kitchen trash, or you *will* regret it. (Pull out the garbage bag and hang it in sight on a cabinet knob. Use it on the day of departure to remind yourself it needs to go out.)
- Only a heathen would leave dirty dishes in the sink for nine days; do yours.
- Put your lights on a timer or use phone-controlled smart plugs. Leave a porch light or bedroom light on (to keep other heathens out).

- Water your plants. Schedule autotimers on your sprinkler or ask a neighbor for an assist.
- If you rent, check that your renter's insurance is up to date, and get clear about what it covers. Consider telling your landlord that you'll be leaving town. It may be a condition of the lease.
- If you're going on a summer trip, set your thermostat to four degrees warmer than usual. For a winter trip, drop it four degrees. (If you turn your HVAC system off entirely, it will need its own vacation after working so hard to come back to life when you get home.)
- Charge your electric car.

Be the award-winning proprietor of the best B&B you've ever stayed at: your own home. "Dang," you'll say when you return, "the management here is on point!"

PET CARE

I got my first dog, Moxie, a tiny bernedoodle, in January 2020. The pre-pandemic puppy purchase may be my most brilliant buy of all time.

Now that I know what true fur-bundled love is, I understand how integral pet care is to the pre-departure checklist. When I head to the Himalayas, Moxie will board with the most loving and responsible honorary pupper-parent in the Pacific Northwest. I've already got it lined up.

Arrange pet care as far in advance as possible. If you've booked flights, it's not too early. Double- and triple-check that your parakeets and iguanas will be looked after. This is what you signed up for when you adopted Twinkie the hedgehog.

Dog owners should pass their fur-children to their most trusted friend, trainer, or doggy daycare rufferee. Simplify the handoff by prepacking food, toys, leashes, poop bags, and your smelliest smock. Make your instructions as easy to follow as your travel plans.

If you have a cat, snake, turtle, or chinchilla, hiring a drop-in pet sitter should suffice. Hand over a house key and tell them exactly what you need. Change the litter on Thursday. Change the water daily. Every Wednesday of the waxing gibbous, drop a mouse into my snake's cage and cover your eyes.

It pains me to recall, but while I was traipsing through Chile in my late teens, my beloved goldfish, Cookie, committed suicide out of sheer neglect. I found him blue and belly-up twelve feet from his bowl on the kitchen floor. I understand if, in light of this confession, you can no longer trust my so-called pet care expertise. I assure you, however, that my loss has only bolstered my commitment to helping pets thrive in their owners' absences. In Cookie's honor, please round out your pet preparations by supplying stand-in caretakers with a list of dietary restrictions, exercise quotas, and emergency contacts.

You could take your pet with you on your getaway, but if they're too squirmy to endure the vet's annual heartworm exam, don't press your luck at passport control in Cameroon.

SELF-CARE

Your trip itself is a form of self-care, but a few moments of relaxation before you get away will center you for the journey ahead.

This may seem futile if relaxing is the primary goal of your trip. If you'll be staying at a resort with a full-service spa for the next week, you probably don't need to take a bath tonight.

No matter where you go or how you plan to spend your time there, you'll thank yourself for taking care of your mind and body on the eve of departure.

Get your groom on. Trim your toenails. I try to shave the night before I fly—one less thing to do in the morning.

Approach your meals the same way. Cook a colorful dish for dinner but prepare breakfast at the same time. Set aside a serving of pitaya for your smoothie bowl. Show me your best overnight oats rendition.

What will make you feel most energized as you embark? Pre-flight exercise stimulates your immune system, promotes circulation, and wakes your brain up, too—exactly what you need to counterbalance the ill effects of air travel. Earn your in-flight inertia. Remember that blood clotting from prolonged stagnancy is a serious risk. A short stretching session is better than nothing.

Pulling an all-nighter would be a blatant mistake, but getting a stellar night's sleep isn't necessarily optimal. If you board your flight to Copenhagen fully rested but land exhausted at 11:00 a.m., you're in for a rough day. Shift your sleep time according to your target time zone. Staying up late to zonk out easier on the plane could help you acclimatize. Enter your flight info on the jet lag app **Timeshifter**, which will create a plan to optimize your sleep, light exposure, and caffeine consumption, starting a few days before departure.

Once you've chugged a gallon of water, disinfected your retainer, and completed your shamanic breathwork, you're good to go.

Security Blankets

Knowing you'll need a pet sitter won't keep you up at night, but not knowing who to call if your car breaks down in the Namib Desert might.

It's even harder to sleep soundly now that quasi-apocalyptic scenarios have become so commonplace.

Face your stressors head-on. A few automated replies, policy refreshers, mayday rehearsals, and booster shots should help. If not, there's always therapy.

ON THE ALERT

Alerts speak for you when you're in the Algarve, speaking Portuguese.

Set an automated email alert to warn people you'll be slow to respond or won't be able to. No one knows when you're getting home. Thursday night? Let's call that Monday morning.

If you're worried about your mailbox overflowing with newspaper coupons, credit card promos, and catalogs you never signed up for, set a mail hold with the postal service.

Arrange for a neighbor or front desk person to guard your precious parcels. If you're embarrassed about how many packages you have scheduled to arrive during your absence, delay your deliveries with the carrier.

There's always the "let it pile up and see if it gets jacked" option. That's the mail prep version of running with the bulls. If you're stupid enough to do it and get gored, don't expect me to feel sorry for you.

Set a travel notice with your bank, so your ATM withdrawal at the grand casino in Monte Carlo doesn't get flagged as fraud.

OUT OF OFFICE

A 2017 survey sponsored by the US Travel Association found that 48 percent of employees gave six weeks or less advance notice for their vacations. Yet 85 percent of managers felt employees were being responsible by giving as much notice as possible and agreed that earlier requests were easier to approve.

Give notice about your vacation a few months in advance, ideally at the beginning of the year. Request the time off before you book any flights or accommodation, especially nonrefundable reservations.

Preparing to take time off isn't just about not pissing off your boss. It's about ensuring that you don't come back to a pile of work the size of Kilimanjaro. Making your colleagues' lives easier before you leave will make yours easier when you return.

A few weeks before your trip, devise a plan to work ahead or delegate tasks to coworkers. Summarize your current projects, their deadlines, and any potential problems you anticipate. Make sure the people covering for you know exactly how to complete the tasks you're handing off. Practice them together, if applicable.

Keep your out-of-office message concise. All you need to say is when you'll be back and who else can help in your absence. If saying you'll be out of the "office" sounds weird because you've been working out of a converted closet since March 2020, just say you'll be away from work or email.

THE GREATEST TRAVEL INSURANCE
RANT EVER RANTED

Who's excited for the rant? I know I am.

Spoiler alert: I actually love insurance—when it works.

When I wrecked my car in an accident that, for the record, multiple witnesses agreed was not my fault whatsoever, and Safeco wrote me a check for the full value of my vehicle, I felt amazing about insurance.

I'll happily pay for peace of mind. That's why I insured my fancy camera and all my lenses for loss, theft, or damage. I feel great knowing my gear is protected.

Travel insurance? I'm not a fan.

Most travel insurance proponents are travelers who experienced some kind of disaster and wished they had been protected. If only they had travel insurance before the pandemic...

But travel insurance policies are littered with pages of fine-print exclusions and limitations, like the one about unforeseen events that voided all pandemic claims because, for the claims to be valid, they needed to be made *before* the pandemic was deemed a pandemic!

Even the expensive Cancel for Any Reason (CFAR) policy add-on, which counts, "I'm scared of going on my trip because I think I might die" as a valid reason to make a claim, pays out only 75 percent of the total trip cost. That's after you spend twice as long as you spent planning your trip exchanging emails and voicemails with insurance bureaucrats intent on squeegeeing every dead bug they can off your proverbial financial windshield.

The only time I've ever bought travel insurance was when I went to Antarctica. My expedition required it. Getting heli-evacuated from polar glaciers will run you about $50,000, not to mention entire Gentoo penguin colonies will collectively roll their eyes at you. I figured I'd cooperate.

So is it ever worth it to get travel insurance? If you were taking an around-the-world trip, some kind of basic coverage to protect yourself against inevitable injuries and emergencies would be a no-brainer. On a 9-Day Getaway, it depends...

First, you should find out if you're *already* covered. Your credit card might partially cover you for trip interruption in cases of appendicitis or typhoon. You might also be able to recoup approximately $12 if your aluminum suitcase gets scuffed.

Familiarize yourself with your credit card's insurance perks. And remember, you need to use the card to book your trip in order to be protected. It might not be the same card that scores you all the bonus points.

Don't count on any credit card to cover flare-ups related to preexisting medical conditions. Same goes for emergency coverage. If you're venturing into the heart of darkness and have a history of epileptic seizures, you might want to pay for insurance. If you're going to Norway and are scared you might fall off your mountain bike, just try really hard not to fall. You got this.

Some people may be tempted to insure their trips against flight changes and cancellations. If you cancel your own flight, you might be at a loss. If the airline cancels your flight, they owe you a new one!

Worried about having to cancel an expensive accommodation if you break up with your partner four days before your trip to South Africa? Pay extra up front for free cancellation. No one wants to read a Moby Dick-sized PDF of insurance policy exclusions, so I'll summarize the gooey part for you: "Unmarried couple arguing about cost of ATV tour" is 100 percent excluded.

What about that add-on option when you're checking out on Expedia or some other booking site you shouldn't be booking on? It looks something like this: PROTECT YOUR TRIP FOR ONLY $29. FRIENDLY REMINDER: ATROCITIES MAY BEFALL YOU. Have fun spending three and half months submitting itemized bills, receipts, and doctors' notes you either lost or never procured to the Expedia Passenger Delight Brigade. They'll be sure to connect you to Tina in Manila who is standing by to initiate your claim. *Tina, are you there? Tina? Hello?*

Travel insurance: the more you need it, the more expensive it is. The less you need it, the more terrified you are into believing you do.

That's it. That was the rant.

PAPER TRAIL

Paper? Are you out of your mind? What is this, 2004?

A hard copy of your passport is a far cry from a nonfungible token. You can't sell it for millions on blockchain.

Yet physical printouts of vital documents remain valuable back-ups in a travel context when digital access can be splotchy.

Create a list of emergency contacts. List phone numbers for your bank or credit cards along with embassy info. Throw in the name of the coffee shop where you might find that tour guide your friend's cousin's friend introduced you to that one time. He knows all the spots.

Perhaps you want to print your entire itinerary and all your reservations. You could put everything in a pretty folder and not have to whip out your phone at every juncture. I won't judge you as long as you feel at ease.

SHOTS IN THE ARM

Vaccines for travel aren't new. Chances are, you've already gotten a few.

Routine vaccines like the tetanus shot, however, require a booster every ten years. If your first reaction is to call a parent and ask how long it's been, you're probably ready to re-up.

Check the CDC for country-specific vaccine recommendations for localized viruses and diseases like yellow fever and typhoid. Get a jump on these at least a month before your trip. Whether or not you get the rabies vaccine, avoid staring contests with macaques at the monkey park in Ubud.

If you're worried about malaria, there are preventative drugs. Side effects include full-body rashes, devastating nightmares, and abnormal fingernail growth. Good luck.

Dengue fever? Don't worry, there's a shot for that. One caveat: it only works on people who have already had the disease.

For all mosquito-borne diseases—malaria, dengue, Zika, West Nile, chikungunya—your best protection is to not get bitten by mosquitoes. Simple! Just lather yourself in 100 percent deet. Convince yourself that it's nontoxic even though it's a pesticide that smells like radioactive waste. Reapply every two hours, don't touch your eyes, and don't breathe.

Now let's address the pangolin in the room.

COVID vaccines, tests, and travel regulations are here to stay. The challenge is no longer getting a vaccine if you want one. It's keeping track of the ever-changing requirements, tests, results, strains, and boosters. Countries have their rules and airlines have theirs. Best-case scenario: the information you find is consistent and up to date. Worst-case scenario: you test positive and are forced to quarantine in an abandoned panopticon.

Expect you'll have to show up to the airport with a negative test for both your outbound and returning flights. Tracking down rapid COVID tests abroad is only getting easier, but you may need to schedule an appointment in advance or factor in wait times for results, which can take twelve to twenty-four hours.

Vaccine passports like the IATA Travel Pass are well-intentioned tools to securely store and manage vaccine and testing certificates. Trust, privacy, fraud, and ethical issues remain serious concerns, but digital green passes are picking up traction and should simplify the health-screening ecosystem.

PURA VISA

Vaccine passports and regular passports aren't your only barriers to entry. You may need a visa to legally enter your destination.

The overwhelming majority of countries do not require tourist visas for US citizens. The ones that do make you jump through a few hoops to get it. If you're lucky, you can apply online for an electronic or printable visa. More likely, you'll need to mail your passport (along with extra passport photos, a printed application, and the requested fee) to the consulate to have your visa glued in. If sending your treasured stamp booklet into the ether doesn't cause you at least a smidgen of anxiety, you're doing it wrong. Don't forget a tracking number.

Double-check that you're applying for the right kind of visa and that your itinerary won't require a special one for multiple entries or brief passage into another country. Get a head start on your application because expedited processing can be pricey and stressful. Consult your target country's embassy site for the latest updates. I have the Uzbek consul's Telegram handle if anybody needs it.

Safe Travels

Thinking so carefully about coming home when you haven't left yet might feel uncomfortable, but your ability to embark in equanimity depends on it.

Create your own plans and procedures to protect your home and health while you're away. There are the things you need to accomplish to not get fired from your job or thrown in quarantine, and there are the things you need to accomplish for your own well-being. Administrative tasks and the general upkeep of your personal affairs are equally essential.

You know your own anxieties and compulsions better than anyone. Maybe you're distraught that you won't be there to celebrate Twinkie's first birthday. Maybe you're worried that your beloved fiddle-leaf fig will wilt. Maybe your only fear is Montezuma's revenge. Acknowledge the source of your unease and make a plan to not let the disaster movie playing in your head become reality.

Failure to lock down the home front makes orderly packing impossible. Once you've handled your business, grab your suitcase, and get your roll on.

CHAPTER 10

Ahead of the Packing

"So throw away your baggage and go forward. There are quicksands all about you, sucking at your feet, trying to suck you down into fear and self-pity and despair. That's why you must walk so lightly."
—ALDOUS HUXLEY

BY READING THIS far, you've proven your willingness to be uncomfortable. With the contents of your suitcase, you have nothing to prove. Be comfortable.

I know it may be hard to reconcile your vision of yourself as a jet-setting fashion maven with the practical demands of a travel wardrobe. But you don't need to be Angelina Jolie on the cover of *Vogue* while in the Sahara. Restraint is often the key.

Asking, "What can I get away with bringing?" is much less advisable than asking, "What can I get away with leaving behind?"

But packing is more involved than choosing which velour tracksuits won't be joining you in Singapore. It's about being deliberate with your choice of bag, efficient in how you fill it, and strategic about making your belongings work for you.

In the Bag

The wrong bag filled with the wrong stuff can make your whole trip feel like one extended CrossFit workout. Snatch the first dusty barbell on wheels that tumbles out of your hall closet. Hurl it into cab trunks. Sling it onto scales and yank it off conveyor belts. Grunt, curse, and sweat profusely the whole time. It's the best workout in town.

Or maybe, instead of working out with your bag, your bag could work out for you. Maybe its style and construction could enhance its utility instead of hindering your mobility. Now we're rolling.

CARRY YOUR WEIGHT

You only have to lose one bag, one time, to be scarred for life. After it happened to me, I went over a decade stubbornly refusing to part with my bag under any conditions. But letting the airline lug your impedimenta for you has its merits. Thus, the carry-on versus check-a-bag debate rages on.

The chief benefit of carrying on your own luggage is agility. The check-in process is faster; you can skip the line and use a kiosk or the airline's app to get your boarding pass.

Another boon of carrying on is not having to wait for your bag at your destination. Some connections require you to collect and recheck your checked bags, which can be stressful if you're tight on time.

Carrying on means you never have to worry about having checked an item you wish you had with you on a plane or during a layover.

People pack for destinations, not airports. When you add it up, it could take a full day to reach the white sands of Palawan. Checking a bag thus requires more mental effort; the personal items you carry on are even more important. If you hand over your luggage, anticipate everything you might need throughout the duration of your travels. Double-check that you have all medications, ointments, gear, extra layers, and stuffed animals you'll need in transit.

Carrying on does require more physical work. You may have to roll your bag miles through labyrinthine international hubs (I'm looking at you, Schiphol) and lift it into overhead compartments.

Many passengers worry they won't be able to find space for their bag. It's a valid concern on domestic flights but rarely an issue on international flights with bigger planes. There's always someone willing to assist.

Perhaps the biggest pain point of carrying on is limiting your cosmetics to comply with airport regulations. In the States, you can bring a quart-sized bag of liquids and gels in your hand luggage, provided no item exceeds 3.4 oz. In most of Europe, there's a 100 ml (about 3.4 oz.) limit per individual object, and all liquids and gels (except medicine needed during the flight and baby food) must fit into a 1 L transparent bag (20 cm × 20 cm). If you're traveling with lots of makeup, sunscreens, pastes, repellants, perfumes, serums, or other elixirs, this could be a carry-on deal breaker.

If this 1 L transparent bag sounds like a bugaboo, one tactic to avoid it is to carry on for your outbound flights and check your bag for your return flights. You can even bring a collapsible third bag if there's a reasonable chance you'll come home with more souvenirs than you can fit in your original bag. Put all the honey you bought abroad, barely used sunscreens, and all your heaviest objects in your original suitcase, check it, and carry on the collapsible bag with any lighter fare that spills over.

Occasionally, you'll encounter an additional security screening at the gate. If you're carrying on a full roller, this can prove especially tedious. It's usually random and can be downright violating. They'll unzip your bag, dig through it, and be sure to snag your most delicate piece of clothing as they zip it back up. Or maybe they'll let you rezip it, which, depending on the fullness of your bag and its inner order, can be exhausting and/or embarrassing.

Ultimately, you must decide if the convenience of having your luggage with you at all times outweighs the inconvenience of lugging it. On a 9-Day Getaway, I always challenge myself to carry on. I encourage you to do the same, without pressing your luck. If your extra personal item is as hefty as your main bag, a check-in agent may force you to throw your roller on the belt. Check the airline's rules if you'd rather not take any chances. In summation:

Carry on if…

- You're terrified of handing over your bag.
- You know you're capable of packing light and want to be unencumbered.
- Your additional personal item or handbag is not enormous.
- You'll have no time to spare when you land.
- Check a bag if…
- You're happy to hand over your bag for minimal schlepping.
- You're unable to whittle down your possessions.
- You packed an elaborate skincare regimen.
- You need to bring a lot of gear: hiking boots, heavy jackets, etc.

SHELL SHOCK

The primary appeal of a softshell bag is that you can squeeze more into it and manipulate it into small spaces. That's exactly why I don't recommend them. I've been the guy surfing on his own bulging bag, trying to cinch the splitting zipper. It's not a good look.

With a hard-shell bag, you don't have any wiggle room to abuse. The expandable feature on a hard shell gives it the Achilles' heel of a soft bag, making it smushy and wobbly like a Bosu ball. Although hard shells may not let you cram as much in, they're more durable.

Soft shells love to add four to seven superfluous pockets. They are better for short business trips, when you're using the bag like a backpack on wheels and want your laptop and personal items easily accessible. On a 9-Day Getaway, when you've packed like a pro, you shouldn't have to open your bag twelve times in the terminal.

Hard shell with no expander for the win. If you want to roll in a different direction, suitcase yourself.

MATERIAL THINGS

Failing to consider what your bag is made of is like a parent failing to consider their babysitter's criminal record. If you're shopping for a new case, you might want to run a background check. Materials matter.

Luxury luggage maker Rimowa started the **aluminum** luggage trend decades ago. Aluminum bags look like safes on wheels, conferring an elite air onto their owners. But they are heavier and can scratch and dent much easier than bags made of other materials. Some travelers treat these blemishes as jet-setter badges of honor. I prefer passport stamps for that.

Polycarbonate is a durable plastic and the best material for hard-shell bags. It has a bit of flex and is extremely strong for its weight. Polycarbonate bags are hard to break and hard to beat for overall value.

ABS is a blend of three kinds of plastic. It's ultralight but not as durable and, thus, cheap. Don't buy a bag made of ABS if you ever plan on checking it or want a bag that's going to last a while.

Polypropylene is another semi-durable and lightweight luggage material, but it can't withstand as much abuse as polycarbonate.

I'm trusting you won't employ some sketchy plastic imposter to protect your precious personal effects.

TRUNK, LOCK, AND ZIPPER

Apparently, they still make two-wheeled rollers. Avoid! It's four-wheel spinner or bust. You have to be able to roll your bag sideways down a plane aisle.

Wheels must pass the cobblestone test. How would your bag hold up if it were bouncing through those streets like a diabolical lawnmower?

Beefy zippers are also essential. A zipper that splits in the middle is the luggage equivalent of an exposed butt crack. A snaggy zipper is the luggage equivalent of GET A NEW BAG. (Or you could try a bag with trunk-style locking clamps.)

Getting a bag with a built-in TSA lock won't hurt, as long as you don't delude yourself that the lock will keep the contents of your bag secure. The locks are worthless against forcible entry and hilariously easy to pick. Besides, TSA master keys are easily downloadable, 3D-printable, worldwide-shippable, and about as hard for criminals to procure as a pile of dirt. TSA locks do one thing well: they keep your bag from falling open on its own. Not exactly the most impressive tech innovation of the century.

BAGS OF TRICKS

Bags are becoming so smart they should offer free Zoom consultations. They've got USB chargers, GPS trackers, digital locks, built-in scales—you name it.

Maybe start with a washable liner and work your way up to Chief Technology Officer. Keep in mind that there are portable versions of most of these smart features that might make more sense for you in portable form. For example, a **power bank from Anker** or **Bluetooth trackers from Tile** (where have *these* been all my life?).

If you don't need Alexa in your luggage, there are some fantastic bags out there for reasonable prices. The first time I traveled with my twenty-five-inch **Delsey Aero** hard shell, the agent at the counter belted, "This thing looks like a Cadillac!" And it still does, after countless conveyor belt beatings (it was $150).

BEHIND THE BACKPACK

My wife looks like a turtle in her travel backpack. Yeah, I said it.

Her carry-on strategy is to get the highest-volume backpack she can find that won't be banished to the cargo hold. She uses it as another suitcase. It's not tall but so deep that she can't turn around without bludgeoning someone with her tortoise shell.

The Spanish word for turtle is *tortuga*, which happens to be the fitting moniker of a respectable backpack brand. **Tortuga** makes 35 L (the maximum international carry-on size) and 45 L (the maximum US carry-on size) backpacks intended to replace rolling suitcases. **Nomatic** is another one-and-done backpack contender that makes a clever 40 L duffel-backpack hybrid.

As a photographer, I travel with a **40 L Ajna pack from F-Stop Gear** but not as a replacement for my primary suitcase. It allows me to safely carry on all of my equipment.

I don't necessarily want to walk around with all of that gear on a given day of my trip, so I travel with another backpack for daily use—a lightweight, collapsible piece that I bring, empty, in my main suitcase. Nomatic partnered with photographer Peter McKinnon to create their **21 L Cube Pack**, a protective camera cube that unfurls into a lightweight, water-resistant backpack. It's the perfect solution to the big-backpack, small-backpack dilemma.

For non-photographers, smaller 15 L–25 L packable backpacks, like the collapsible **technical packs from Matador,** are ideal for short adventures.

Of course, your backpack choice comes down to how you intend to use it. On second thought, forget backpacks. Everyone on earth should wear a fanny pack.

The Things You Carry

In 2013, I lugged a pack full of energy bars and endurance goos to the summit of Mount Rainier. I was *prepared.* But when my group hit the high altitudes, trail mix tasted like dirt. I felt like I was eating a bag of pebbles.

My guide, meanwhile, pulled out a Costco-sized bag of Mike and Ikes and passed it around. Candy was the perfect antidote to the harsh conditions. It gave us an energy boost and the sensation of being in a movie theater rather than roped together on a frigid volcano. The lesson was obvious: to pack well, bring not only what you'll need but also what you know you'll want.

Ask yourself, what are you going to wish you had? A snack, supplement, or sugary indulgence? A dressy pair of shoes? It may feel silly to schlep your go-to protein powder all the way to Bhutan. But I, for one, would be stoked to drink a protein shake in Thimphu.

How you pack is just as important as what you pack. You've got an airtight itinerary and a ten-day weather forecast. Now, to master prudent, organized packing...

A FINE TIMELINE

- **One week out.** Pull out everything you think you want to bring. All the summer shorts you want, all the hats you're excited to rock, all the T-shirts that feel suited to your destination. Gather the contenders and assemble them into piles, sorted by category.

- **Throughout the week.** Refine your selections. Look for redundancies and possible eliminations. Then gradually rein it in to your final picks.
- **Two days out.** Aim to be fully packed. Since there's a 4 percent chance that you will be, rejoice that you tried and keep moving. If it's 2:38 a.m. and you're still obsessing about whether to bring sandals or boat shoes to Malta, get a grip and go to sleep. Obviously, sandals.
- **The night before.** Worship your *Do Not Forget* list. This is the final checklist you'll confirm is fully crossed-off as you walk out the door, and it consists of those straggling, hard-to-remember items. Your favorite pair of pants drying on the line. Your glasses on the nightstand. Your Flintstones vitamins. Your full heart.

POUCH CITY WELCOMES YOU

I wasn't always an expert packer. Then I married a professional organizer. She taught me the wonders of pouches, and I realized my belongings had been sloshing around all willy-nilly like a chewed-up hamburger in an empty stomach.

Now I have a sun-protection pouch and an insect-eradicator pouch. I have a pouch for my coins, cards, and cords. I have a pouch for my street clothes and one for my undergarments. My packed suitcase is a finished puzzle. Pouches are the pieces.

Pouches keep the contents of your bag neat, compact, separated, and easy to find. No more digging through your bag like a burrowing chipmunk. That's not classy.

Two dependable pouch pioneers are **Flight 001** and **Eagle Creek**. Both brands make an array of useful travel organizers, from garment sleeves to shoe cubes, toiletry kits, and tech cases. Flight 001 pouches have vent holes to facilitate compression and dual zippered sections provide a built-in way to separate clean and dirty clothes.

LIQUIDS AND GELS

Toiletries can be the biggest bottleneck in the packing process. They always seem to screw up the lofty dream of being fully packed the night before. That's why so many people forget their toothbrush or deodorant on trips. The items you use on the day of departure are the easiest to forget. (I repeat: *Do Not Forget* list.)

Whatever toiletries, makeup, or medicine you decide to bring, and whenever you decide to pack it, first things first: decant. Use refillable, airless pump bottles or **GoToob silicone bottles**, especially if you're carrying on. You can also look into purchasing travel-sized versions of the cosmetics you use. Often, these can be refilled, and they'll be easily identifiable.

If you're going to Sardinia and forget sunscreen, no big deal. You'll get some when you're there. But certain personal care items, if forgotten, can crush your ability to enjoy a trip.

There's nothing I'm more terrified of forgetting than my contact lenses. You don't want to see me without my contacts. I look like a drunk zombie who just got pepper-sprayed.

Oh, sure, I could wear my glasses for nine days straight. And then I could wear my sunglasses over my eyeglasses. How cool would that be? The four-lens look is trending right now.

Not quite. Take extras of any items you couldn't replace on the road. And to be safe, keep your extras separate. For example, I keep some contacts in my Dopp kit and some more in my backpack.

Bring a smaller cosmetics bag of essential items to freshen up in transit. Even if you carry on, keep this mini pack separate from the rest of your toiletries, in your personal bag and not your primary suitcase. At a minimum, this should contain a toothbrush, toothpaste, and deodorant. You may want to throw in face wash or wipes and moisturizer.

This easy-access vitality pouch is even more necessary if you're checking a bag, in case your luggage is lost or delayed.

CLOTHES MINDED

Packing goes awry when people try to get too clever. Bringing a silk couture bodysuit when what you really needed was a pair of jeans. Bringing three pairs of jeans when what you really needed was…a pair of jeans. Bringing a Canada Goose parka instead of a collapsible Uniqlo puffer. Overloading on jewelry. Skimping on undies.

The key to packing for a 9-Day Getaway is versatile layering. You need hardworking pieces that play in a lot of situations. Pieces that match and fit with each other. Pieces you could happily wear several times between washes. Lightweight pieces that clean easily and dry quickly.

More fail-safe packing guidelines to streamline your process:

- Choose polyester or nylon blends, or best of all, merino, instead of cotton. Merino wool doesn't dry as fast as synthetic fabrics but resists odor and regulates body heat.
- Always bring one obligatory warm item. Wear it on the plane along with your bulkiest pair of shoes and other heavy garments.
- Heavy items are not your friend. Leave your duck-cloth shirt-jacket and corduroy trousers at home unless you're boarding for Helsinki.
- Remember to pack activewear. Nobody wants to zipline through the jungle of Costa Rica in selvage denim.

- Just having a general sense of the climate isn't sufficient. Cue up that Doppler radar and get the specifics you'll need to inform your travel uniform.
- Decide how many times you can rewear an item without washing it before feeling grotesque. You're not engaging in a vague process but rather a counting game. Count an outfit or two for each day of your trip and add a count for every rewear.
- Focusing on outfits, not items, will keep you honest. That shirt doesn't go with any of your pants and therefore has no place making the cut.
- Avoid one-wear, dry-clean-only pieces. An exception would be if you needed a more formal outfit for a dressier dinner. Aim for one or two of these pieces max.
- Remember, there are packable versions of most items, including parkas, rain jackets, and sun hats.
- Pick a palette. It doesn't matter what it is, but sticking to one color palette will ensure your pieces pair well together.
- Be selective with accessories. These are your chance to add spice to your fits. They should complement almost everything you're bringing.
- Check Pinterest for location-specific outfit inspiration. Emulate or take inspiration from example packing playbooks.
- If you're stuck, talk it out with someone. They may be able to spot redundancies or oversights.

You've designed an itinerary that takes most of the guesswork out of the situations and conditions in which you're likely to find yourself. Pack costumes to match the stages you'll be performing on.

WASH AND LEARN

The golden packing question: Will you have an opportunity to do laundry at any point on the trip? Access to laundry can halve the quantity you need to pack.

If not, clean socks, underwear, and T-shirts become precious commodities. Yes, you can bring packets of detergent and wash your own clothes in the sink. But will you? And if you do, will they actually come out clean? There's something about that cursory hand-washed after-musk that makes "clean" clothes, now greased with Tide residue, feel dirtier than they were before. Yummy.

If you have a free- or low-hassle opportunity to wash clothes, take it.

My Airbnb in Dubrovnik, the last stop on my 9-Day Getaway to the Balkans, had a washer. One small load of laundry ensured I had fully clean base layers for my journey home through Amsterdam.

Hotel laundry service is a mixed bag. I needed a refresher at the Grand Hyatt in Muscat, Oman, a beachside Biedermeier bastion befitting a Wes Anderson film set. I'd just spent a night at a tent camp in the Dubai desert. The sand was atomic, the finest I've ever felt. Walking on it was like walking on melted butter. By the time I got to Oman, I had moondust spilling out of every crease and crevice of my bags.

In my air-conditioned hotel room, I still felt like I was camping. I found a laundry bag in the coat closet, dumped half my suitcase into it, hung the bag on the outer door handle, and called the cleaning staff to request a pickup. The next morning, my clothes were returned to me, devoid of dust, perfectly folded, nothing shrunk—brand new! Only when checking out did I discover that my zesty Omani swagger had cost me US$180.

There are other more cost-effective options. Most places feature a laundromat. You'll be tethered to it for a few hours, but if it's located in an interesting area, you can use the time to explore the vicinity.

SHOES TO FILL

How many pairs of shoes you bring on a 9-Day Getaway, and what types, depends on your destination. Call it one to three—a comfy walking and workout shoe, something dressier for dinners out, and a sandal or casual slip-on for hitting the hammam at the Hotel Tremezzo.

If you're a one-and-done kind of gal or guy, make sure your selection is versatile and endlessly stylish. Either Vibram FiveFingers or snakeskin cowboy boots.

Your shoes must go in their cube or shoe bag unless you want to smear the petri dish that is their soles all over your clean undies. Sneakers are cooler and more acceptable than they've ever been. A solid color option can reasonably get you from the museum to dinner to breakfast the next day.

It's Electric

The in-flight entertainment system boasts over three hundred movies. But you forgot the two-prong adapter to plug your plush headphones into the plane's dated screen. Have fun binge-watching Marvel blockbusters with a death-gripping disposable foam headset whose volume never tops a whisper.

Enjoy your road trip through the countryside. Pump up the jams. Oh, wait. Your phone is dying, and you forgot a power bank. Luckily, there's a convenience store up ahead. Maybe they'll have a cigarette charger. And an aux cord. Wait, what do you *mean* there's no Bluetooth in this 2012 Mitsubishi Mirage?

The right electronics can supercharge a trip. The wrong ones can fry you. Let's get plugged in.

POWER PLAY

Easy access, high-capacity charging is essential on the road, especially if you'll be depending on your device's battery-draining GPS to get around. Carrying a portable charger allows you to recharge in transit without having to constantly scavenge for outlets.

I recommend the **Anker PowerCore 20100 mAh** for a powerful all-purpose charger. Anker also makes a slimmer **10000 mAh version**, but unless you're diligent about recharging your portable battery every night, a more powerful charger is a safer bet in foreign territory. Just remember to bring your own cord if the model you select doesn't include one. **Anker's nylon-braided PowerLine cables** are more durable than basic cords, which I stopped buying altogether after learning the hard way that they are not puppy-proof.

A portable surge protector is another travel essential. I recommend the **360 Electrical PowerCurve Mini 3.4**, which turns a single outlet into two rotating outlets and two USB ports. I love being able to charge my laptop, camera, phone, and power bank at the same time. But even with extra outlets and protection against voltage spikes, you're still going to need an adapter.

SOCKET TO ME

Travelers are in a tizzy about adapters and converters. I don't know if it's a fear of getting electrocuted or embarrassment about not knowing the difference between the two, but I'm here to assure you, it's not that complicated.

Different countries use different plugs. An *adapter* allows you to plug your country's plug into another country's socket. To figure out what kind of plug adapter you need at your destination, visit worldstandards.eu.

You can either get an all-in-one global adapter (a brand called EPICKA makes a popular one), which are chunkier but will prevent you from ever having to think about adapters again, or a single region-specific adapter, which is less bulky but requires some sleuthing to ensure you bring the right one.

The term *converter* refers to a voltage converter. There is no standard global voltage. The voltage of your appliance must match the voltage of the country you're visiting. Otherwise, you're going to plug in your American hair straightener, and it's going to make a lightning noise, erupt in smoke, and die.

I have fond memories of this happening to my sister on family trips. I never imagined that an appliance could produce a worse smell than that of her burning but immaculately straight hair every day, but the even more toxic electrical-fire smell of the straightener short-circuiting takes the cake.

The United States uses 110–120 volts. Same with Canada and most of Central and South America. Outside of the Americas, every other country in the world (besides Japan, Taiwan, and Liberia) uses 220–240 volts.

The key question is, is your appliance *dual voltage?* This means that it can accept both 110–120 V and 220–240 V. My sister's 120 V hair straightener was no match for France's 230 V current, hence the fumes and disgruntled shriek emanating from our shared hotel room's water closet.

To check the voltage of a certain appliance, read the fine print on its charger. Look for "100–240 V" or "120/240 VAC" to confirm that it is indeed dual- or multi-voltage and will function abroad without a converter.

Great news, though: practically every modern device, especially larger ones like laptops or cameras, is dual voltage. It's usually smaller or older appliances, like sleep machines and hair dryers, that aren't.

Adapter: essential. Converter: not as much.

CLICK BAIT

"What camera should I get?" is one of the most common questions I receive about trip planning. I wouldn't recommend the same trip to every traveler, and the same is true for cameras.

Where, when, and how do you intend to use the camera? When I created my fine art photography store, **2STRAWS Print Shop**, my travel camera requirements changed significantly. To make high-resolution prints, I need a full-frame camera with a massive sensor. If I just wanted to send a few 8 × 10 prints to my mom, a 61 MP camera would be excessive.

Are you more inclined to take stills or video? Are you looking for a cheap point-and-shoot, a high-end compact, an interchangeable lens camera, a professional rig, or an action cam? These questions will narrow down your selection process.

Even more important than the camera you take is that you know how to use it. Consider renting a camera or lenses from your local camera shop before going all-in on a hefty purchase. You may find the equipment is too complicated for your proficiency level. Or you could rent a Sony G-Master 70–200 mm f/2.8 for your trip to Iceland, fall in love with its telescopic sharpness, and buy it before your expedition to Antarctica.

I shoot with a **Sony A7RIV** and highly recommend **Sony's A7** lineup and other offerings, from the pocketable **RX100 VII** to the more versatile **A6600**. I prefer mirrorless cameras to DSLRs because they're generally lighter and more compact.

As for lenses, nothing beats a zoom for travel. When I want to take only one lens on a trip with me, I bring a 24–70 mm. If you intend to shoot animals (I would never!), you'll want at least a 100 mm lens. Ideally, you could capture both wide-angle and telephoto images without having to change lenses in the field.

Before you tumble down a camera rabbit hole, one final consideration: Do you need a "real" camera at all? Your phone can speak to you, spy on you, and direct you to the nearest bakery. Its camera may be sufficient.

Bring It!

Your best effort, that is. Not your zip-off pants. You can leave those.

If you dread packing, it's likely because it forces you to confront the preexisting disorder in your home or head. The dread of facing that disorder only makes the job harder in crunch time.

Decanting, dividing, deciding…these are tolls you happily pay on the highway to freedom.

Packing is a privilege, not a predicament.

You get to travel wherever you want and bring (almost) whatever you want.

You have time to select the luggage most appropriate for your journey.

You have the itinerary and information you need to fill your bags deliberately.

You have the knowledge to never let gear and gadgets intimidate you again.

You know where you're going, why you're going, and what you'll do when you get there. There's only one thing left to do.

Go.

PART 2

TAKING THE TRIP

CHAPTER 11

Own the Airport

"If we are always arriving or departing,
it is also true that we are eternally anchored.
One's destination is never a place but rather
a new way of looking at things."
—HENRY MILLER

THERE'S NOWHERE QUITE like airports. On the one hand, they're launchpads of adventure, gateways of discovery, and fascinating foci of progress and opportunity. On the other hand, they're claustrophobic corrals wherein someone's child is always throwing a tantrum, someone else is conducting a business sales call at maximum decibel levels, and a bottle of water will set you back $7.99. And let's not forget the lines.

But there are tricks to take the stress out of the airport experience. Here's how to tame the terminal.

Checking In

Your airport ownership commences the moment you arrive.

163

If you're checking a bag, you may not even need to bring it inside. Curbside check-in, while not available for every airline at every airport, is still a viable option to expedite the ticketing process. The service is usually free, although some airlines charge a few bucks per bag. Tipping skycaps is customary. Tip generously if you are traveling with multiple heavy bags.

Speed through the check-in process by doing as many tasks in advance of your arrival at the airport as possible. These can include checking in electronically to get a mobile boarding pass, paying luggage fees if you're checking a bag, and uploading negative COVID test results.

Do not be a sheep. Don't stand in a line just because others are. Have your wits about you. Look for self-service kiosks and bored ticketing agents loitering behind counters.

Rushing to make your first flight is a form of self-punishment. Being late is so much more miserable than being early.

Airlines recommend arriving at the airport three hours before international flights. Two and a half hours of leeway is usually plenty to avoid a sprint relay to your gate.

Breezing Through

It's hard to believe that before 9/11, airport security was run by private companies. You could bring a box cutter through security with you. A bottle of water! If only passing through checkpoints in an international terminal today were so easy...

You can't circumvent the typical airport kerfuffle. But you can avoid falling victim to it. With a few fast passes and a dose of determination, intentional travelers will blow past every administrative blockade.

GOING GLOBAL

Global Entry is an expedited immigration and customs program run by US Customs and Border Protection (CBP). It allows you to skip the regular immigration line (most of the people on your flight) and walk straight to a Global Entry kiosk. You scan your fingerprints, get your photo taken, and hand over your printed receipt to a CBP officer. This can be the difference between a thirty-minute wait and a two-minute ID check.

Breezing through immigration is delightful, but I especially enjoy competing with myself to see how ugly my kiosk photo can be. The photo of me after my Sydney to Los Angeles flight, in which one of my eyes is rolled back as if I were passing out, remains my most abominable mugshot.

Global Entry is rolling out facial recognition, but regardless of how they screen flyers, there is a serious speed advantage of skipping the ordinary passport control line. Global Entry also grants you access to the fast lane at customs (after you collect your luggage, when they ask you if you brought any seeds back from Amsterdam).

The cost of membership is $100 for five years. The fee includes **TSA PreCheck,** which costs $85 for five years, so there's no reason to choose between the two. Pay the extra $15 for Global Entry to unlock the benefits of both programs. If you already have TSA PreCheck and decide to join Global Entry, you'll still have to pay the full $100.

Global Entry requires an online application and in-person interview, which can be a nuisance. The enrollment centers are usually located inside the airport, on the stealthy second floor of the terminal that you never knew existed.

If you object to making a special trip to the airport to get photographed, fingerprinted, and interrogated about your criminal background (it's not that bad), you may prefer the Enrollment on Arrival option. It's the same process but allows conditionally approved applicants to complete their interviews upon arrival into the United States. I imagine only someone who pours their milk before their cereal would find this option appealing.

REALITY PRE-CHECK

Would you pay $85 for five years for the right to keep your shoes and jacket on and leave liquids and electronics in your carry-on bag while you go through security? I would encourage any frequent traveler to do so.

The Transportation Security Administration (TSA) introduced PreCheck in October 2011 to pre-screen "Trusted Travelers." Like Global Entry, it requires fingerprints and a background check. Apply and schedule an enrollment appointment at tsa.gov.

Can you be trusted to make the obvious choice and enjoy a dedicated fast line at domestic security checkpoints forevermore? Remember to add your TSA-assigned Known Traveler Number (KTA) to your reservation in order to reap the benefits.

EXTRA CREDIT

Some credit cards reimburse cardholders for either Global Entry or TSA PreCheck every four to five years. The **Capital One Venture Rewards Credit Card** and **United Explorer Card** are two such cards with relatively low $95 annual fees. Popular premium cards such as the **Chase Sapphire Reserve**, with a $550 annual fee, and the **Platinum Card** from American Express, with a hefty $695 annual fee, also offer the perk. If you're considering signing up for a new travel card, keep this credit in mind.

UPWARDLY MOBILE

For anyone on the fence about Global Entry, there's one more option for expediting the immigration process upon arrival: **Mobile Passport.**

This free app, authorized by US Customs and Border Protection, allows users to fill out the customs form digitally and show a QR code instead. No more desperate digging for a pen on the plane.

The free version of the app doesn't save your passport info. You'll have to pay $14.99 per year (with a free trial) or $4.99 per month (with no free trial) to store your info. Even the premium version requires you to fill out the digital form each time you reenter the United States, in the brief window of cell reception between landing and entering the immigration area.

You should see a designated Mobile Passport line, although they can be hard to find due to poor signage. These lines only operate as smoothly as the airport personnel who oversee them. Many Mobile Passport users complain of airport personnel using them to accommodate spillover from the normal line or wheelchair passengers, which can negate the speed-boost you signed up for.

The free version of Mobile Passport could be sufficient if you don't envision traveling enough to warrant the higher cost of Global Entry or if you're trying to make a tight connection. But Global Entry is still the more expedient and dependable option.

CLEAR THE AIR

CLEAR is like a remote Mediterranean island rapidly gaining in popularity but still underappreciated by the masses. After one visit, you realize you've discovered something special but hesitate to share the booty. Thankfully, there's enough booty to go around.

CLEAR's biometric identification kiosks and designated lines let you skip the entire security line. You'll flash your boarding pass at the TSA agent, who will wave you through with languid nonchalance.

When the poor chap who had just waited forty-five minutes in the slow line realizes you sidestepped into his lane without even showing your driver's license, he'll glare. At this make-or-break moment, you can either feel guilty for "cutting" the line or smile graciously, knowing you paid for and are entitled to the service you received. Salty slow-line guy will live. And you'll get through security in under three minutes.

Signing up for CLEAR is simple. You start the enrollment online, complete it at any US CLEAR location, and you can use it immediately.

You'll have the choice of scanning your irises or fingerprints. I've always preferred the fingerprint scan because I'm terrible at staring directly at lasers without it feeling like I'm staring directly at lasers.

My favorite aspect of CLEAR is that you can combine it with TSA PreCheck. Using the two in tandem keeps you from having to strip down to your pajamas before shuffling through the metal detector.

The annual membership is $179, but there are easy ways to save. Delta SkyMiles and United MileagePlus members pay a discounted rate of $119, and flyers with status on either airline pay $109. TripIt Pro members are eligible for a four-month free trial. Students get the best membership deal: $50 per year.

Lounging Around

When you have a long journey ahead of you, nothing is more valuable than peace, privacy, and personal space.

Lounges provide all three, along with services and amenities that, elsewhere in the airport, are expensive, inferior, or hard to find. These include complimentary food and snacks, refreshments, Wi-Fi, TVs, newspapers, magazines, office areas, massages, and sometimes—my favorite—showers.

The first time I ever took a shower in an airport was at the Air New Zealand lounge in Sydney. I was about to board a fourteen-hour flight to Los Angeles. I had showered that morning and didn't need to take another one. But I wanted to experience boarding a flight feeling brand new. I liked lounges before, but after that experience, I realized just how revitalizing they can be.

Lounges are places to spread out, relax, check in with friends or family, and take a moment to appreciate the ritual of traveling.

So how do you get in?

GET CARDED

Premium credit cards may have high annual fees, but they'll make you a VIP at the airport.

The **Amex Platinum Card**, one of the best overall cards for lounge access, grants cardholders access to **American Express's Global Lounge Collection**, which includes Amex's own network of **Centurion lounges**, access to **Delta Sky Club** lounges (when you're flying Delta), and over a thousand other lounges across a handful of partner networks, including **Priority Pass**.

The **Chase Sapphire Reserve** and **Hilton Honors American Express Aspire Card** are two other premium cards that come with a Priority Pass Select membership.

Airline credit cards often give users access to that airline's lounges. For example, the **Citi/AAdvantage World Elite Mastercard** grants access to **American Airlines Admirals Club** lounges, and the **Delta SkyMiles Reserve American Express Card** grants access to Delta Sky Club lounges.

These premium cards come with a slew of other benefits, but if you travel frequently and want a plush terminal experience, their lounge perks alone make them worth acquiring, or at least considering.

THIS TOO SHALL PRIORITY PASS

I waited to board my flight from Papeete, French Polynesia, to LAX. The open-air terminal was sweltering, seating was minimal, and I sat on the sticky floor thinking, *There has to be a better option.* I saw a discreet staircase in the corner of the terminal and climbed it out of curiosity. How convenient—a Priority Pass lounge.

Priority Pass is a global network of over 1,300 lounges in over 600 cities. Almost any airport in the world in which I happen to find myself has a Priority Pass lounge.

Premium credit cards are the best way to secure membership, and almost all cards that include the perk allow up to two complimentary guests.

You can also buy a Priority Pass membership the old-fashioned way (where you simply pay for something, rather than paying for something that includes something else but may or may not include other things. Read the fine print if you can find it. Good luck). The Standard Priority Pass membership costs $99 per year plus $32 per visit.

Be warned: Priority Pass lounges regularly deny access or limit their hours due to space constraints. If you ever get denied, feel good about being a member of such a coveted network. But if you're counting on a particular lounge being open—"If I don't steal a Saran-wrapped red delicious apple from the Euphoria Room in Terminal C, I'll *literally* die"—double-check availability on the **Priority Pass** app ahead of time and/or pray.

BUDDY UP

Want lounge access but don't have the right credit card or Priority Pass? You can buy a day pass. These passes cost between $25 and $75 and can be worth it if you have a long layover and find a lounge with showers and unlimited food and libations. Although you can pay at the door, you'll likely save by booking in advance with an app called **LoungeBuddy**.

American Express purchased the free, à la carte lounge-booking app LoungeBuddy in 2019. The app lets you browse lounges and compare their perks. Add your elite statuses and number of guests to determine what lounges, if any, you have access to.

Infrequent travelers might prefer LoungeBuddy over Priority Pass for one-off lounge access, but Priority Pass members could still benefit from LoungeBuddy if they get denied at a Priority Pass lounge and want an on-the-fly replacement.

The **American Express Green Card** offers a $100 credit for LoungeBuddy bookings, but that will only cover a few lounge visits and might not be worth its weight in pasta salad.

STATUS SYMBOL

Earning elite status with an airline or alliance, and the lounge access that comes with it, requires flying a certain number of miles or segments in a year.

If you're nowhere close to attaining elite status, you can always get the royal lounge treatment by flying in first class.

Your last option is to buy an annual pass to an airline-specific lounge for $350–$550. Unless you're a very frequent flyer, I advise against this method. You'd be better off with a premium credit card.

PRACTICE SAFE CHECKS

Having access to a lounge in any airport is a worthy goal. But start by guaranteeing lounge access at your home airport. Find a list of all lounges at your home base. Which lounge are you most likely to need and use?

Check in advance that there's a lounge where you're flying. Make a note of its location. Visiting a lounge is almost always worth it, unless you have to traverse three wings of a sprawling international terminal to reach it and will have only fifteen minutes to spend there, shoveling as many rice crackers and macarons into your piehole as you can fit without feeling like a freeloading glutton.

Boarding Soon

With or without lounge access, you can still maximize your time in the terminal.

Instead of sitting mindlessly at the gate waiting for the agent to announce your boarding group, use the downtime strategically to further prepare for the plane.

If you didn't yet, download your airline's app. You may need it to access onboard entertainment. Also download any music or podcast episodes you'll want to listen to in the sky.

Airport restaurants charge premiums to their captive audiences and are generally inferior to their out-of-airport locations due to staffing and delivery challenges. If you need to eat, find a happy medium between fast food and a $19 plate of romaine lettuce. There's no telling what heinous crimes Shake Shack and Nathan's Famous hot dogs may commit on your stomach after takeoff.

The **Grab** app lets you order airport food from your mobile device and could save you time otherwise spent queueing with fifty fellow passengers all quivering with anxiety that they won't get a Potbelly sandwich in time for their flight.

If you're not overly concerned about finding space for your bag in the overhead bin, there's no rush to board. Bins do fill up, but note that newer planes have larger compartments and may decrease the odds of you having to shove your overstuffed bag under the seat in front of you and pretend your legs fit, too.

Some frequent fliers prefer to board last and spend as little extra time on the plane as possible. I like to board right away to give myself ample time to disinfect my entire row with Clorox wipes.

The official airline recommendation is to be at the gate forty-five minutes before departure. I would advise you to be in the vicinity, at least, so you don't miss important flight updates. You may need to flash your passport to a gate agent or open your bag for a final inspection. Use the restroom and fill up your water bottle at a filtered fountain one last time before you enter the jet bridge. Please don't pay $8 for an eleven-ounce bottle of Fiji water.

Come Fly with Me

We can't all be Leo DiCaprio as Frank Abagnale Jr. in *Catch Me if You Can*, strutting through Miami International Airport in gold-rimmed aviators and a double-breasted blazer to a crooning Frank Sinatra soundtrack. We may not look as gleeful at the check-in counter as the white-gloved Pan Am flight attendants on his arm. But the heyday of air travel is not in 1965. It's ahead of us.

Airports are evolving from mere hubs into architectural marvels and becoming destinations unto themselves. Terminals of the future will offer more of all the amenities passengers crave, while deflating every tension point. There will be more lounge and gate capacity, more open spaces, more connections to nature, improved light and air quality, auto-tinting windows for heat and glare regulation, state-of-the-art baggage handling systems, simplified wayfinding technology, and enough robots to make you wonder how much longer we'll need pilots. Don't expect them to let up on cleanliness anytime soon either. Electrostatic disinfectant mists, UV-blasting droids, and touchless versions of everything are the new norm.

These are places you're going to want to spend a lot of time. You're going to want to take the stairs instead of the elevator. You're going to feel like you're in an oasis. You may not want to leave.

If airports don't make you feel like this yet, focus on the variables you can control. Reenergize your mind and body instead of chomping on chili cheese fries. Sure, my fellow passengers may look at me funny when I perform a vinyasa flow or interpretive dance at the gate, but when we get off this ten-hour flight, I'll be a supple panther, and they'll be kicking themselves (or trying to) with their unbending legs, wishing they'd lubricated their hip flexors before departure. Hashtag synovial fluid.

The time you spend in airports is growing increasingly valuable. Whether it's a fleeting connection in Cleveland or extended stopover in Singapore, if you're in the terminal, your getaway has begun. So, too, has your mindful travel performance.

Honor your terminal time the same way you honor your trip time, because it's all the same. Besides, what's the point of making the airport your playground if not to feel your best before you step on the plane? With a proactive attitude and strategic plan, you can sail through security, glide through immigration, and genuinely enjoy the airport experience.

You should have time to spare to clink mimosas before you board.

CHAPTER 12

In Plane View

"I fly because it releases my mind from
the tyranny of petty things."
—ANTOINE DE SAINT-EXUPÉRY

AIRPLANE VICTIM IS such an easy role to master. You sit there
and whine in silence until they let you off, numbing your brain
with worthless entertainment or trying stiffly to work, in a privacy
vacuum, at the germ parade, inside a used toilet paper roll with
wings, but metal and bumpy, yet trustworthy, you hope. Greg, the
pilot, a voice, nothing more, blares pleasantries while new neighbors crack their teeth on chem lab wasabi peas washed down
with concentrated juice, and are blown away by farts unheard, yet
smelled, and misassigned to you, but no! you swear! You do have
to pee. Could they let you out of your seat?

But there are two ways of seeing yourself on an airplane:
trapped or free.

Physically, you may feel trapped, caged in like a hen destined
to lay pale eggs.

In truth, in flight, you are liberated. Soaring above the clouds? That's angel territory. And in a world where there's so often somewhere you'd rather be, being confined to one space propels you into a state of presence.

It may not be the gentlest entry into be-here-now bliss, but while your butt is in that seat and there's nowhere else to go, your mind can become as birdlike as the plane with its own chance to fly.

Take Comfort

Staying comfortable on an airplane, even in the most expensive seat, is challenging. Your skin gets dry, your feet swell up, it's loud even when it's quiet, and nobody gives you good chocolate.

You must resist all of the invitations to turn into a warthog. Ideally, try to stand up and perform some light stretches or bodyweight exercises once per hour. The occasional round of torso twists, leg swings, calf raises, and a front-folding hamstring stretch will keep you from morphing into a head of wilted lettuce.

If you're wedged into a window seat and don't want to stand up to go to the gym in the galley, at least pull your knees to your chest and shake out your feet.

Step your neck pillow game up. You deserve a nillow (coming soon to a *Merriam-Webster* near you) with a high-rising collar-to-jaw cushion and foam dense enough to support your snoozing skull. Try the **Cabeau Evolution** or **Travelrest** memory foam offerings. Avoid the mushy newsstand pillows with the little beads that collapse under the weight of your chin, shock you with static zaps, and sound like a steeply tilted Peruvian rain stick.

The least you could do is wear compression socks. Find a moderate (15–20 mmHg) or firm (20–30 mmHg) sock like the full-

length options from 2XU and just say no to deep vein thrombosis.
If you've never changed your shirt two-thirds of the way through a flight because you never remember to bring a change of shirt because you don't see the value of changing your shirt, treat yourself to the incomparable luxury of a mid-flight freshie.

Herd Immunity

There's no one-size-fits-all approach to boosting your immune system while you travel. My arsenal contains:

- **Liposomal vitamin C,** as a general infection warder-offer. I use the Lipo-Spheric travel packets from LivOn Labs.
- **Liposomal glutathione,** for detoxification and cell protection. I like Glutathione Force from Bulletproof.
- **Elderberry,** to protect against viruses and inflammation. I'm a fan of the Sambucus gummies from Nature's Way.
- **Vitamin D3,** to decrease your susceptibility to infection. I like the 5,000 IU softgels from NatureWise.
- **NAC,** a potent, free-radical scavenger. I prefer the 900 mg capsules from Pure Encapsulations. Note: NAC supplements may be hard to find on Amazon after a recent nitpick from the FDA.
- **Oregano oil** from Gaia Herbs, for respiratory health and cold prevention.
- **Propolis** from Beekeeper's Naturals, for its antiviral compounds.

I also like to round out my collection with a few drops of colloidal silver, a couple of pellets of activated charcoal, two masks, and a face shield. Airborne pathogens can't tell me nothin'.

Please consult your own naturopathic doctor—I am not one—when designing your in-flight supplement regimen.

Hygiene Freak

It's hard enough not to catch a virus. You also have to prepare your body for the dehydrating assault of a low-pressure airplane cabin, the equivalent dryness of air at 8,000 feet.

Skin routines are like fingerprints: everyone's is different. But dermatologists, aestheticians, and style bloggers all agree: your plane face needs moisture.

Try to walk on the plane with your serums and goops already applied. Wash your face immediately before your flight, then begin to build an impregnable moisture fortress on your skin. Bolster your battlements with a vitamin C serum for ultimate antioxidant defense. Toughen your turrets with hyaluronic acid, which attracts and retains water. Build a moisturizer moat around your facial castle with your most protective cream, ideally one with SPF. UV rays take no prisoners at high elevations.

The jury is still out on the efficacy of in-flight skincare as opposed to preflight protection. Some beauty gurus swear by mid-flight Korean sheet masks, while others argue that your dewy, nutrient-laden skin will turn your face into a breeding ground for all the germs you were trying to avoid. I once used a sheet mask on a long-haul flight from Dubai to Seattle. I felt like Jim Carrey in *The Mask* and frightened a few fellow passengers, but it did feel amazing. Nonetheless, given the implausibility of wearing both a luxurious beauty mask and the now commonplace germ-catching variety, I'd wait until you land to self-administer any such expert aesthetics.

Lip balm, eye drops, and hand cream should round out your kit. Some travelers like to dab Aquaphor or Neosporin in the edges of their nostrils to prevent cracking and create a final barrier for germs. Makeup or body wipes may also come in handy, especially if you get carried away on sleeping drugs and wake up in a cold sweat.

It's not illegal to reapply deodorant on a plane. You're also allowed to brush your teeth, although I wouldn't dare swallow or even rinse with lavatory sink water, which makes LA tap water look purer than the freshwater in Torres del Paine.

A 2019 study released by the Hunter College NYC Food Policy Center uncovered some murky truths about plane water quality. Federal regulations require airlines to routinely collect bacteria samples from their aircrafts, and the required sampling frequency increases the more often a plane's water system is disinfected. But the minimum disinfection frequency is only once per year. Airline violations of the Environmental Protection Agency's Aircraft Drinking Water Rule (ADWR) have declined since the rule's implementation in 2011. There's no telling whether this decrease in violations is due to stronger airline compliance or weaker EPA enforcement. Either way, the EPA doesn't test plane water according to its own National Primary Drinking Water Regulations (NPDWR), which limit a smorgasbord of other contaminants in addition to total bacteria. Ask any flight attendant. They don't drink water from the plane's festering tanks. That means a hard pass on coffee and tea.

It doesn't mean don't drink water. In fact, drinking a lot of filtered, non-plane water is the best way to take care of yourself in flight. Avoid caffeine, alcohol, and salty foods which will only dehydrate you more. Choose an aisle seat so you can guzzle a full Hydro Flask without concern for your bathroom-use frequency.

Let nothing come between you and freakish aerial hygiene.

Let Me Digest

Flying wreaks havoc on your gut. The low pressure on planes practically shuts off your digestive system and forces it to work even harder when you land.

Instead of gorging yourself on the plane, try to eat two to three hours before your flight. Stick to magnesium-rich foods like leafy greens and seeds, which help relax muscles and keep things moving. Unlike sugar, healthy fats like nut butter, coconut oil, and avocado will give you the necessary nutrients and long-lasting energy you need to reach your destination without falling into torpor. Oranges are another dependable preflight snack for their high-fiber content. Pineapples may be an even better fruit choice. They contain an enzyme mixture called bromelain which improves digestion. If you really want to show off, soothe your stomach with a fennel or peppermint infusion.

Avoid any foods that cause bloating at sea level, because the bloating those foods induce will only get worse in the air. "Jet bloat" is yet another airplane condition that makes us feel wonky. We swell up in the sky. Our feet feel tight in our shoes, and all the air in our bodies expands. Beans, broccoli, cauliflower, and cabbage are major preflight no-nos. Carbonated drinks won't do you any good either.

Do yourself the courtesy of bringing your own in-flight nosh. All aviation experts know that airplane food has only one ingredient: regret.

Do you have any idea how far in advance those meals are prepared? Long enough to give them the shelf life of canned tuna. And you know how canned tuna works, right? You only eat it if you're a bodybuilder who just survived an earthquake. And that's about the only person to whom I'd recommend eating the overly salted, offensively sauced "food" they serve on planes.

But airplane food doesn't suck simply due to desperate preservation attempts. Airlines actually trick us with their recipes. In
2010, the Fraunhofer Institute in Germany conducted a study,
commissioned by Lufthansa, to test passenger sensitivity to certain foods while flying. As cabin pressure throws our mucus mem-
branes out of whack, we lose around 30 percent of our sensitivity
to sweet and salty foods. Airlines douse food with even more salt
and sugar to make us think we're not actually eating reheated
sloppy joes drenched in canola oil.

Paradoxically, some foods taste better on planes. Tomato flavor
is enhanced in the sky, as are savory umami notes, which is why a
Bloody Mary tends to be one of the most popular cabin cocktails.
Knowing this, airlines try to spruce up their in-flight meals by
smothering them with copious herbs and edible unguents. You
may notice beers infused with berries and honey, and deceptively
fruity wine. Save your taste buds the hassle of demystifying these
laboratory concoctions and don't eat or drink them.

Perhaps the best reason of all to fast on the plane is to prevent
jet lag. In 2009, Harvard neuroscientist Dr. Clifford Saper studied
"master clocks" in mice and concluded that there are two internal
clocks that tell mice and humans alike when it's time to eat and sleep.
One, of course, is light. But another clock can override our biologi-
cal clock—which can take days to adjust to new time zones—and
force us to adjust almost immediately: hunger. Dr. Saper argues that
a sixteen-hour fast is the most effective jet lag remedy of all, as it
stimulates a tiny cluster of brain cells (the dorsomedial hypotha-
lamic nucleus, if you must know) responsible for circadian activity.
Essentially, when you're fasting, you become hyper-alert and don't
care whatsoever that it's 4:00 a.m. in Kuala Lumpur.

Without fasting, you can still put your gut in position to succeed
by taking a probiotic supplement like **Mt. Capra Caprabiotics Plus**

or **Vitamin Bounty Pro-50.** You could also bring a tub of sauerkraut on the plane to get your fermented food fix, but there are better ways to make friends.

Water is just as essential to in-flight digestive support as it is to skin health, immunity, and hygiene. If you opt to fast, **Branched-Chain Amino Acids (BCAA) from Kion** can keep you from feeling like you're wilting away. Travel packets of **Athletic Greens**—packed with antioxidants, digestive enzymes, vitamins, and adaptogens—are a fantastic, albeit pricey, way to load up on micronutrients pre- or mid-flight. **Nuun hydration tablets** will give your H_2O a boost, as will a few squirts of **electrolytes from TB12.**

One final piece of advice: no matter how desperate you are for potassium or vitamin C, never travel with a banana. Not all peelable fruits are created equal. Some are firm; others become pudding in the crevices of your weekender bag, are forgotten, and grow mold (I should have just eaten the damn thing). Treat "banana" in this ancient proverb as a euphemism for any seemingly innocuous travel aid whose benefits aren't worth the mess it might make. Airplanes have enough mushy food on them already.

Sleep on It

I've never had much trouble sleeping on planes. But that was before the mask era. I usually wear my eyeglasses instead of contacts, so my eyes don't get dry, but the glasses-mask combo turns me into Fogzilla. The cloudy vision flusters me, which makes me breathe like Darth Vader, which intensifies the fog.

Normally, I'd don an eye mask, something silky, breathable, and contoured that didn't smush against my eyelashes. But the eye mask-face mask combo is only a half-step away from Egyptian mummification; at that point, I might as well throw a towel over my face like I just lost a championship.

My all-time most effective plane-sleeping technique is to wear a baseball cap and drape a lightweight mid-layer over it like a beekeeper's net. A cotton-linen blend. I pitch my own little tent over my face. It doubles as a Do Not Disturb sign. What flight attendant would ever tap the shoulder of a man cocooned in such an intricate homemade sleeping bag to ask if he cared for cranberry juice or ginger ale?

My sleeping veil barely touches my head at all when I'm wearing my **Bose QC35 II headphones** underneath. The QuietComfort noise-cancellation is so good that I sometimes turn them on even when I'm not listening to anything, simply to drone out the rumble of Boeing engines and have a polite reason to ignore people.

If bulky headphones aren't your style, consider simple foam earplugs to give you the false impression that the toddler sitting in the row behind you is not, in fact, wailing.

Insomnia-busting apps like **SleepStream 2** or meditation apps like **Headspace** and **Calm** could help facilitate your catching of Zs. Also consider downloading a playlist of solfeggio tones or "sleep frequencies" on Spotify before your flight. Your cortisol levels will plummet.

Everyone has their own go-to sleep concoctions: Ambien, Dramamine, red wine, CBD oil, reishi mushroom extract…Whatever sleep-enhancing recipe you cook up, avoid any drugs or supplement combinations that could keep you comatose after you land.

Cabin Fever

Buying special supplements, sleep aids, skin creams, and stomach soothers may seem like a lot of work. But your plane ride is the gateway to your getaway, and flight-induced digestive, muscular, circadian, and immune system ailments could linger for days after you land. Why risk it?

No matter what defenses you put up, a long flight will always knock a few of them down. By nature, plane travel disrupts all of your normal cycles. That's why it's so important to prepare for the inevitable punches planes throw at you.

If you're content with letting free radicals usurp your wondrous body, or allowing your bowels to shrivel up and knot, or permitting your skin to impersonate an iguana, or being more disoriented when you hit the ground than a concussed wide receiver, then by all means, ignore the advice you just read.

Conscientious voyagers won't be content unless they touch the tarmac with their bodies and self-respect intact. You'll want your faculties as sharp as possible when the captain turns the seat belt sign off. That's when it's really time to buckle up.

CHAPTER 13

Ground Control

"This is a great moment, when you see, however distant, the goal of your wandering. The thing which has been living in your imagination suddenly become part of the tangible world. It matters not how many ranges, rivers or parching dusty ways may lie between you; it is yours now for ever."

—FREYA STARK

THE INITIAL MOMENTS when you land in a new country are among the most exciting of any trip. When I first step outside the airport terminal, I'm usually so giddy I feel drunk.

As the buzz wears off, health and safety regain their rightful priority. The most serious threat you face is not the aggressive taxi driver whose vehicle reeks like a frat house and resembles a wheeled armadillo. It's your own complacency.

Adjusting your body and behavior to meet the demands of your destination is not a passive process. It takes commitment and vigilance to feel good on the ground, protect your personal property, and navigate the ultimate hazard: other people.

Check Yourself

Brain fog. Insomnia. Lethargy. Constipation. All of the above. How are you supposed to look alive if you feel half-dead?

Imbalances after a grueling day of travel can spiral out of control if you let them. Physical ailments make you irascible and impatient—the worst kind of tourist—and an ill-timed outburst abroad can be not only embarrassing but dangerous. Move with purpose to find your rhythm.

COOL YOUR JETS

You need a proactive plan to fight jet lag if you want to stand a chance.

Adjusting your sleep schedule in the days leading up to your departure and changing your watch the moment you get on the plane are good starts. The earlier you begin operating in alignment with your target time zone, the better.

To prevail, follow the sun. Light exposure tells your brain it's time to boogie. If you land in Reykjavik at 8:00 a.m., go straight outside. Soak up some rays with your shades off. If you land in Geneva at 6:00 p.m., stay indoors, away from windows and You-Tube, with your blue-light glasses on.

If you need a pick-me-up, nothing beats a cold shower to kickstart circulation, release endorphins, and make you hate yourself and feel invincible in a thirty-second span. Bonus points for doing exercise first. Save the hot shower for when it's 3:00 a.m. and you're playing imaginary speed chess with shadows on the ceiling. A few milligrams of melatonin won't hurt either.

Personally, I'm better at staying awake when I'm tired than going to sleep when I'm not. Whichever way your body clock betrays you, there's one more circadian ace to play: earthing, aka grounding.

There's a reason why walking barefoot on the beach, doing cartwheels in a field, or planting star jasmines in the garden makes us happy. The earth charges our cellular batteries. In flight, we overload on positive ions, which increase inflammation. Negative ions in the ground neutralize our charge and bring us back to equilibrium. This is great news because it means you just got permission to sprawl out on that narrow patch of grass behind the hotel parking lot for the next twenty minutes, indifferent to the piercing stares of passersby who assume you must have smoked grass before you dug your toes in it.

WORK IT OUT

COVID taught millions of people how to get a complete workout in the privacy and confinement of their own homes. Space and equipment are exercise luxuries, it turns out, not necessities.

If you really want or need to, you can get an excellent workout without leaving your hotel room, using only your body weight and some creativity. It may not be the Zumba, CrossFit, or hot yoga class you're used to, but it will count. Jumping jacks, squats, tricep dips on a desk chair...Don't act like you can't break a sweat when what you really mean is you just don't feel like it. Check out an app called **Freeletics** for bodyweight training inspo or **Alo Moves** for functional fitness flows.

Bring an exercise band for resistance training in small spaces or a thin jump rope for an anywhere, anytime cardio blast.

Try to get your exercise outside. Running or biking through a new city are exhilarating ways to survey your destination when you first arrive. Use the **Strava** app to discover and map your route. The Strava Local feature shows you popular runs and rides in your area but sadly does not pin the locations of any doughnut shops.

Utilize the terrain or architecture at your destination to customize your workout to fit the setting. Swim in a lake. Pretend you're an Olympic volleyball player and run shuttle drills on the beach. What unique features of your destination can you take advantage of to get an even more dynamic workout than you could at home? Walk uphill on an unpaved path. Hiking, they call it.

If you are committed to duplicating your home workout routine abroad, I commend you for your dedication. But please relinquish any expectations that your P90X core circuit will go off without a hitch. You may slide around too much on the carpet of your hotel room or encounter a glitchy connection when you try to stream your dance class.

Good news for any stragglers who neglect fitness altogether on their trip: you'll probably still come home five pounds thinner and lighter on your toes than a toreador, simply by having walked nine miles a day for nine days.

Safe Hands

The consequences of losing your passport or having it stolen could be the difference between a 9-Day Getaway and a new permanent zip code. It is imperative that you safeguard your stamp collection.

For starters, pencil your address and contact info into the emergency contact page. To ensure no one ever sees that page, keep your passport in your hotel room. A copy will suffice when you're out and about, filling out a VAT refund form, for instance, or booking a tour (but keep your driver's license on you).

For a forgetful person, there is ironically nowhere more dangerous to put valuables than in a safe. Instead, bury your passport in a secret backpack pocket, or secure it in a portable safe like the **PacSafe Travelsafe GII**. You can also request that the front desk hold your passport for you. Just make sure they remember to return it to you when you leave.

If you're worried about people seeing the cover of your passport, realizing you're American and despising you for some heinous foreign policy you had nothing to do with, you could get a passport holder. One quick tip about those protective leather booklets: never give your passport to an immigration official while it's wrapped in one. They'll scorn you far more for the inconvenience of handling it than for your inexplicable obsession with football.

Speaking of sports, you may want to conceal your allegiances, not because anyone cares what teams you support but simply not to look so…foreign. Don't turn yourself into the kind of oblivious tourist a pickpocket or other criminal would be keen to take advantage of. Shopping bags, ironic T-shirts, and spinning in circles while pointing all put the target on your back.

Money belts may not be the latest streetwear trend (on second thought, they may be), but they work. Zip-pocket pants also help guard your wads of baht, kunas, pesos, or pounds.

THICK AS THIEVES

A friendly stranger in San Telmo gestured to the camera dangling around my neck. He looked very concerned.

In that Buenos Aires neighborhood, he explained, bad things happen to tourists with big cameras. Armed robberies and assaults were not uncommon.

I put my camera in my bag and took it out again only to snap a photo in the colorful La Boca neighborhood. Another friendly stranger, another stern warning: put the camera away!

Gotcha. Buenos Aires: not the safest place for street photography. But I should have known that before any locals had to warn me.

The threat of violent crime may not be so severe in other parts of the world, but petty crime is a risk everywhere (including home).

Thieves are waiting for you to let down your guard. Set your phone on the bar. Rest your bag against your legs under the café table. Put your suitcase on the train seat across from you and nod off. Even when you're on high alert, a simple smokescreen can be enough to distract you. A spilled drink. Papers flying. A scuffle. A fracas.

Tethering yourself to your belongings in public helps. At least twist your backpack strap around your arm or pin it under the restaurant chair. Prevent your wallet and phone from bulging out of your back pocket where they'll stand out like gold bullion.

Research common scams in your destination. Don't let anyone sell you a ring they conveniently found on the ground beneath you, or put a bracelet on your wrist, or pass you a clipboard.

The most effective scams are the ones that tug on your heartstrings. But not every child and elderly person begging for money has pure intentions, and their solicitations are often ploys. Either way, think twice before flashing money in vulnerable communities (or anywhere in public, for that matter).

Your desire to help is noble, but you'd likely make a bigger impact by donating to a local organization. Consider volunteering with **Give a Day Global**, which matches travelers with nonprofits for one-day opportunities, or **GivingWay** for a short stint of voluntourism. (Manatee rehabilitation in Belize, anyone?)

So if you can't help an old lady who trips and falls because she might be a ruse, and you can't give money to a poor child because she's been trained to lift wallets, and you can't ask the smiling latte sipper at the adjacent table to watch your laptop while you use the restroom, who *can* you trust?

Trust yourself. Trust your instincts. I learned the hard way. Trust me.

PRAWN QUEEN

Mozambique's allure is mostly phonetic. It has a "z" and a "q" in it. So does "quiz," but Mozambique doesn't pop. So does "quartz," but Mozambique doesn't shine.

My sister and I came for more than the country's sexy name. In the capital, Maputo, there's a fish market, and in that market—so I heard—they sold prawns the size of bananas. I had to see these succulent oversized crustaceans for myself.

The market crackled. Fish piled on bare wooden tables with no ice or prices. Maputo survives on the day's catch. I didn't know what kinds of fish I was looking at, but they were thick, raw, whiskery, and diverse. Mounds of pink, fleshy squid. Buckets of floating clams. It was the Times Square of seafood—everything freakishly oversized. I gaped at predatory crabs with claws like eagle wings. I had no idea I was looking at lobsters until I saw the bottom of a cardboard box, which I had assumed to be lined with a turquoise-patterned cloth, squirm. They were two feet long and decorated with what appeared to be zebra stripes, polka dots, and rare gemstones. They looked like rusty toucans. I had never seen creatures like this before.

The prawns surpassed my hopes. One whole branch of the market was devoted to them. They soaked in massive red and blue barrels. They were eight inches long and marvelous.

A few women had a monopoly on the whole Maputo prawn circuit. They knew exactly how much to overcharge tourists—

a price commensurate with our excessive enthusiasm. We approached the prawn counter with raised eyebrows, making awe-stricken sounds like crashing waves and pointing stupidly. We might as well have shown up tarred and feathered with dollar bills instead of feathers. The Prawn Queen knew exactly what to do with us.

"We want prawns," I said. "Jumbos."

She picked up her best-in-show specimen from the top layer of her bucket and stretched it out in front of me. It could have been a foot long.

"Big prawn," she said.

"Yes," I said, "very good." I asked for a kilo.

She reached into her bucket with both hands and plopped a heap of prawns into a brown paper bag. We paid the equivalent of US$10 for over two pounds of prawns, which, in my hungry daze, and compared to American prices, seemed like a steal.

The center of the market transformed into an outdoor dining area with plastic chairs and tables draped in floral vinyl. We negotiated to have the prawns prepared for us and waited for them in the courtyard.

We popped up to greet our feast. But there was nothing whatsoever jumbo about the prawns. They weren't even prawns; they were shrimp. Pygmies. The size of my second smallest toe. Tiny little shits that barely qualified as seafood. They didn't even taste good.

I barreled back to the sorceress.

"I'm mad at you," I spit, waving one of the marine gherkins in her face. "This is not a tiger prawn!"

"It's a mix, it's a mix," she said. "Some tiger, some no tiger."

"All no tiger!"

She shrugged remorselessly.

The woman had tricked us right before our eyes. In one swift scoop, she had reached down to the bottom of her prawn bucket and dropped a kilo of her least desirable supply—buried under the beast prawns—into our bag. We should have pointed to our selections one by one. We should have been watching closely. Instead, we fell for the trick as hundreds, maybe thousands, of naive tourists had done before us.

I still want my money back.

LAST LOOKS

Jackets in restaurant booths. Debit cards in ATM slots. Books in seatback pockets. I've literally left it all on the table.

These scatter-brained incidents feel like gut punches and can put a major damper on an otherwise well-oiled trip. But I haven't left valuables behind (knock on wood) since I implemented one simple policy. It's called The Check.

Do The Check, or "D the C," is a foolproof mantra for not being a careless moron.

Before you leave ANY place—room, seat, car, table, beach, or bathroom stall—you check it *thoroughly* for anything you may have left behind. I know. *Such* a groundbreaking concept.

Even going to a different section of a place, the front of a ferry or lobby waiting area, warrants D'ing the C.

Checking out of a hotel means Doing the Check in your hotel room. Inspect all surfaces. Yank up the sheets. Look under the bed. Make sure your wedding ring didn't camouflage into the bathroom countertop.

Cab ride? D the C. Phones blend into seats. Coats slide off them.

Restaurant? D the C. Glance under the table and at chairs you didn't use.

Stopped moving for longer than a minute? D the C. The habit may spare you both financial damage and emotional agony. On the road, if you lose an item, it's usually gone for good.

The Wrong Crowd

In the mornings during peak season, tour buses flock to the village of Margarites, on Crete, for its pottery. Ceramics shops and studios sell hand-thrown pieces made with clay sourced right there in Rethymno province—perfect keepsakes from an island celebrated for its preservation of ancient traditions. The village I encountered had all the charm I'd hoped it would. We arrived around 5:00 p.m., right when shops started to reopen after the afternoon siesta. We had the whole village to ourselves.

I entered a potter's airy studio as she glazed a mug. Sitting on a stool against the far wall, she was so enthralled in her work that she didn't even glance up to greet me. She worked calmly, trancelike, indifferent to the passing of time. It seemed she had been sitting on that stool, caressing that cup, since the Minoan age—if not her, then some maternal ancestor, a peasant girl born and reborn to perpetually spin the wheel.

Each studio I entered transported me further back in time. With no other tourists gawking, complaining, or otherwise disturbing the serenity of the village, the place was magical. At the local taverna, we enjoyed a prime courtyard table with a panoramic view. I ate the village delicacy, goat stewed in wine, with stuffed zucchini balls. We were the only patrons. Suffice it to say, the service was excellent.

I use the speckled ceramic cup I purchased from the ageless potter's shop as a toothbrush holder. Every day, I'm reminded of the peacefulness of Margarites—a feeling I can only hope to recapture in other far-flung corners of the world.

TOUR BUSTED

One of the best reasons to plan your own trip is to earn the luxury of seeing the best sights without a stampede of tourists trampling ahead of you.

I got a photo in front of the Taj Mahal with no other people in the shot because I resolved to wake up earlier than everyone else and be the first person through the gate. Sometimes, though, simply eating an early dinner or taking a shorter siesta can unlock moments that would never have been possible if you were following a typical tourist circuit and schedule.

I've been on my fair share of tour bus trips. Everything takes so much longer than it needs to. Just getting everyone on and off the bus eats up time I'd rather spend exploring. To dine or shop, you have to wait in line behind all the other people you're traveling with. You have no control over the timing of anything, can't leave a place sooner if it doesn't appeal to you, and can't stay longer if you don't want to leave. The tour bus itself is an apt metaphor for the kind of trip you're likely to have while riding one: slow and impersonal.

If expediency is your aim, avoid tour buses at all costs. Of course, if the attraction is notable enough, you won't be able to avoid large groups. If you pull up to the Great Wall of China parking lot and see fifty buses, you aren't necessarily in the wrong place. You may just be there at the wrong time.

MY GREAT OCEAN NEAR-DIVORCE

Annie and I visited the famous Twelve Apostles on Australia's Great Ocean Road at the worst imaginable time. We were simply cruising along the coast. Whenever we arrived, it would be lovely. Or so I thought.

It was the complete opposite experience of Margarites, and I knew instantly that we'd made a mistake. Hundreds of tourists poured out of buses, doing all the most infuriating tourist things: halting in the middle of the congested walkway to take a selfie with nothing more than bathrooms in the background, blocking the prime view spot to Instagram the horrible selfie they just took, and bumping into strangers while shouting to locate their wailing toddler. It was also 100°F outside, which conveniently attracted swarms of gargantuan horseflies. Perfect.

Annie wanted to turn around immediately. I insisted that we navigate the obstacle course of tourists and insects. I just wanted one quick photo of the Apostles, and then we could head straight back to the car. I didn't realize at the time that I was doing the travel equivalent of what a poker addict does at a casino—ignoring all common sense, refusing to fold doomed hands, and only leaving the table after incurring severe losses.

There they are. The Twelve Apostles. Hooray. Okay, let's get the hell out of here.

I've never seen Annie walk as fast as she did on the way back to the car. She paraded upstream through the rush of meandering tourists. I would have lost her in the crowd, but every time I almost did, I looked for the backhanded swatting motion of her pale white arm, like a spasmodic windshield wiper blade wiping dust out of the sky.

When we reached the car, I was getting major "I could divorce you right now for putting me through that" vibes and wisely decided not to speak. It was such an unfortunate pitstop at such a supposedly unmissable attraction. The real tragedy of the afternoon was not the eroded limestone stacks that seemed to be crumbling before our eyes into the frothing teal ocean. It was my own insistence that we lay eyes on them at all costs. I'd justified the visit by telling myself I'd regret coming all the way to Victoria without at least catching a glimpse of the iconic cliffs.

It is this mentality that dooms so many trips. Not seeing a major attraction is not necessarily a failure. The value of an attraction is subjective and conditional. The pleasure derived from wandering in ethereal Greek light through a serene Cretan village may far surpass the pleasure derived from swatting flies for survival at an overpopulated pitstop.

You and you alone—not a guidebook or travel blogger— determine what is not to be missed. Although attractions are often impressive, they may not be meaningful and right for you.

Street Cred

No matter what valuables you idiotically leave in the hotel safe, or what insufferable tourist traps you suffer, or how much your exercise routine unravels, you can always look back at the determination it took to get where you got and appreciate the beautiful absurdity of your realized dream.

Just don't fool yourself into believing suffering of any kind on your getaway is inevitable. If your body feels confused and your brain feels foggy, fight back. Let your freedom of movement and thirst to explore be your weapons. It's okay to be tired, but it's lame to be lazy.

If traveling mindfully means tapping into a state of awareness, then street safety is as mindful as it gets. Mindfulness means being aware in the present moment, but it also means paying attention when the prawn lady pulls a bait and switch. The same level-headedness that keeps your pocket from getting picked also keeps you in the flow of your trip.

Foreign places have a tendency of disarming you in your most vulnerable moments. Flocks of oblivious tourists are bound to test your patience. Make the necessary adjustments. Adapt to stressors, avoid the hordes, and look alive.

If you already lost your wallet and don't want to talk about it, skip the next chapter.

CHAPTER 14

Smart Money

"Travel is never a matter of money, but of courage."
—PAULO COELHO

WHEN I WAS eighteen, my family traveled to Morocco. In Marrakech, my dad took me to La Mamounia, one of the fanciest and most famous hotels in the city. We popped into the hotel casino, found a roulette table, and scattered a few chips.

I started winning and couldn't stop. Every spin, I got a hit. I walked in with twenty bucks and walked out fifteen minutes later with a couple of hundred, professing my adoration for North Africa.

The next day, we explored the souks surrounding the bustling Jemaa El-Fnaa. I found a shirt I liked and asked the price. It translated to US$15. I felt invincible from the prior day's lucky streak. More importantly, I didn't care that much about the shirt. So I threw out my counteroffer: $3.

The shopkeeper recoiled, flabbergasted at my offensive lowball offer. Holding the shirt out to show me its high-quality fabric and stitching, he asked for $12.

During the exchange, I decided two things. First, based on the signals Marrakech had been sending me, I was a winner. Second, in that instance, winning meant mastering the negotiation.

"Five," I said.

He was beyond insulted, but I could tell he was putting on a show.

"Ten," he said. "Best price."

I examined the shirt one more time, acknowledging its decent quality but not projecting an iota of desperation. I expressed my disappointment that I would not be able to leave Marrakech with the garment. The price was simply not acceptable.

"I won't pay more than six," I said.

He waved his hands and hung his head. I shrugged and turned to exit the stall.

"Eight! Eight! We have a deal!"

I walked out of his shop and into the rush of the medina.

"Six okay!" he shouted after me.

I paid him and took the shirt.

Defining what winning means for you is the secret to mastering money abroad. It could mean leaving a souk with the tunic of your dreams or not sacrificing your bargaining power by failing to conceal your excitement when you find it. Spending more for quality could be a victory. Saving a boatload on something you didn't need could be a loss.

Travel brings money decisions to the forefront because every expense is new. Making the right decision involves weighing your priorities and circumstances. The bargain rental car might not have the handles or horsepower your road trip demands. The private daybed at your hotel pool could be exactly the rip-off you think it'll be. If you can be ruled by something other than the bottom line, that's a privilege that I encourage you to graciously exercise when appropriate.

I'd wish you luck at the tables, but you won't need it if you follow these smart practices for withdrawing, exchanging, spending, and protecting your cheese.

Swipe Right

I recommend using a credit card whenever possible on the road, under one condition: it's a card with no foreign transaction fees.

One of the most popular credit cards with no foreign transaction fees is the **Chase Sapphire Preferred**. I primarily use my **Chase Ink Business Preferred** card, which pays three times the points on travel with no fees.

By paying with a credit card, I can still earn points like I would back home. It's also convenient for keeping track of your spending.

If you're paying with a credit card and are prompted to choose whether to pay in your native currency or the local currency, choose the local currency. That way, your bank will determine the exchange rate, not the merchant, and you'll get a more favorable rate.

Cash Flow

Despite my allegiance to credit cards, I advise always keeping some local currency on you. Small vendors often don't accept plastic or charge customers more to cover fees.

Your overeager self might be tempted to exchange money at the first currency exchange kiosk you see in the airport upon landing, but resist. To ensure the best rate, use an ATM.

Be prepared for ATMs to charge you their own fees and your bank to tack on another fee on its end. For example, Bank of America charges 3 percent on foreign currency withdrawals. That really grinds my gears.

Ideally, withdraw cash with a debit card that won't charge you fees. The best checking account for traveling is the high-yield checking account from Charles Schwab. Schwab reimburses all ATM fees at the end of the month. Pair that with a fee-free credit card, and you might finally stop bleeding money abroad.

Making larger, infrequent withdrawals is a smart way to avoid ATM fees if it's your only option, but carrying gobs of cash can be risky. Plus, if you don't spend it, you'll be tempted to exchange it back into your native currency at the end of your trip, taking another hit via a lousy exchange rate.

Always get more cash when you leave big cities and head to smaller, more isolated areas, where you likely won't use ATMs or credit cards. Keep a small reserve stashed away, separate from your wallet or money belt, just in case. Pay with the smallest possible bills so you don't get shortchanged.

Pro Tipping

Tipping etiquette varies enormously by country. Do not assume that tipping customs are similar in countries that are similar in other ways. Research the etiquette at your destination to avoid the awkwardness or embarrassment of over- or under-tipping.

Tipping is a lot like getting dressed for an event. Underdressing is usually worse than overdressing. But sometimes, looking too fancy just makes you feel like an asshole.

Double-check if gratuity is included on your restaurant bill. Also check the protocol for tipping taxi drivers, maids, and porters.

Refund while It Lasted

VAT, or Value-Added Tax, is a refundable tax available to travelers to the European Union (EU). Not all shops offer VAT-free purchases. There may also be a minimum transaction threshold to qualify for the VAT refund. But if you do qualify, you could save some good money.

Unfortunately, you can't just pay the VAT-free price at the point of purchase. You have to jump through some hoops to get the refund.

The process starts at the point of sale. When purchasing clothes or items you intend to take home in your personal luggage, request VAT-free documentation from the vendor. (You'll have to show your passport. A copy of your passport usually works.)

At your final point of departure out of the EU (train station or airport), you'll need to find a customs office to get your paperwork stamped. At airports, these offices are usually right before the entrance to the security line.

Some VAT-free vendors use intermediary services with their own stands in the airport. Depending on which option the vendor chooses (ask when you pay), you may have to track down the intermediary's refund counter. Thrilled to get your VAT refund yet?

After presenting your unused goods (don't wear your new Fendi bag into the customs office) and receipts to the customs agent, you'll have the option to receive your refund in cash, on the spot, or charged back to your credit card if you originally used one. If you take the cash option, you'll pay a lousy exchange rate to convert the refund to USD. Ideally, pay with a credit card and get the refund electronically.

The process could take anywhere from fifteen minutes to an hour. The refund could take months to reach you, electronically or by mail. And here's the kicker: sometimes it never arrives!

So when would it ever be worth it to endure this bureaucratic rigamarole?

When you've made some substantial purchases and there's big money on the line. You may be entitled to up to 27 percent back.

Having Leftovers

Before I delve further into the topic, I should acknowledge that the annoyance of dealing with foreign currency typifies the concept of "first-world problems."

How hard life is, when you're fortunate enough to have traveled to another country, and then return home with its money still in your possession!

Now that we've gotten that out of the way, we can feel less like spoiled children when we complain about rampant foreign currency.

Hidden in drawers and zipped pouches everywhere are stashes of alien funds. Where's this from? Is that real money, or did you frequent a Chuck E. Cheese and depart with unclaimed prize tokens? Do you even know how much it's worth? What are you going to do with it? You have options.

I. MAKE CHANGE WITH YOUR CHANGE.

If you happen to catch a flight home on one of the many airlines UNICEF has partnered with, you'll have the opportunity to donate the remainder of your foreign currency to the Change for Good program, which provides lifesaving services for the world's most vulnerable children. A lovely flight attendant will walk through the cabin to collect your now mostly useless coins.

Current partner airlines include Aer Lingus, American Airlines, Asiana Airlines, Cathay Pacific, Cebu Pacific Air, easyJet, Hainan Airlines, Japan Airlines, QANTAS, and Tianjin Airlines.

If you've long since deboarded, fear not: you can Change for Good via mail.

That's right, just send your leftover shekels to:

UNICEF USA
Attn: Change for Good Program
125 Maiden Lane
New York, NY 10038

2. TAKE IT TO THE BANK.

Most national banks will exchange foreign currency for their customers. Call up your local branch to confirm. No promises on the exchange rate you'll get, but you might be past caring about that anyhow.

3. MORE COFFEE FOR ME (YOU).

Gauging how much local currency to keep on you as your trip dwindles is a delicate science. You don't want to head to the airport with nothing left because of snacks and coffee. Then again, there's no way to perfectly tabulate how much you'll spend on bags of nuts and stupid magazines. But back to the coffee.

I can't remember the last airport I was in that didn't have a Starbucks. And you know what happens when you load currency onto a Starbucks card? You have money on a Starbucks card that you can use wherever there's a Starbucks. You're welcome.

Keep enough cash on you to tip the hotel maids and catch a cab to the airport. Having leftover foreign currency is better than running out too soon. If worse comes to worst, you can always return to the places you loved and spend it.

WORTH EVERY PENNY

The descent to the village of Lindos on the island of Rhodes was painless. With gravity on our side, we bounded down the sun-drenched road. The way back was a different story.

We found ourselves staring into the gauntlet of trekking back up the ultra-steep, winding road, overflowing on both sides with sunbathers and tour groups.

The taxis wait all day for people like us: sweaty, panting, and holding 1.5-liter water bottles with only a few sips of water remaining. We weighed the absurdity of taking a cab ride up a hill with the severity of our heat-induced delirium. Daring ourselves to be outlandish, we flagged a driver.

The man floored it up the curvy road, which had no lanes or sidewalk, coming so close to pedestrians that I thought he would clip one. He bolted up that hill with such maniacal resolve that in any other circumstance we would have been terrified. Thirty seconds and five dollars later, we were spit out at the top of the road, utterly elated.

I'm sure the other tourists lunging up that final stretch as our lightning-taxi whizzed past them mumbled insults to us. "Those lazy schmucks," they must have said. Back in our air-conditioned rental car, we agreed it was some of the best money we'd ever spent. Shamelessly indulgent and flagrantly unfrugal, it was our most expedient path to freedom and therefore priceless.

How you spend your money abroad is entirely your choice, but the line between paying for convenience and saving for inconvenience can be as thin as a roulette chip. Small indulgences can have big payoffs, and big indulgences can cause more aggravation than they're worth. Small withdrawals can come with hefty fees, and big purchases can come with hefty refunds. You could win big at the casino today but get swindled in the souk tomorrow.

Smart spending and savvy money management won't save you from the jealous barbs of thirsty beachgoers when your taxi blows by. You may haggle your heart out and still overpay. That's life. If you ever need to tally your gains or losses, at least find reliable Wi-Fi.

CHAPTER 15

Well Connected

> "Almost everything will work again if you unplug it for
> a few minutes, including you."
> —ANNE LAMOTT

THE NOTION OF totally unplugging on a trip is admirable. Without internet, you're more likely to forget or release the responsibilities and stressors of home and work and immerse yourself in your immediate experience. But internet and screen time can also eliminate most of the stress of navigating foreign places, and potentially help you stay on top of your obligations at home.

I support and encourage a predesignated "unplugged day" (or days) on which you abstain from using your phone. On my favorite, achingly charming island, I leave my phone locked away in my hotel room. Yes, it's hard. Occasionally, I cheat. But when I truly unplug, it feels amazing.

You could download an app to automatically lock your phone or intentionally drain the battery, but those methods are no match for willpower. I once tried rubbing toxic varnish on my cuticles to stop biting them. After ingesting the finger poison a few times, I simply stopped applying it to my nails.

More realistic are self-imposed usage limits, such as checking your phone only in the evening, or to help you track down the next train from Tokyo to Fuji Five Lakes.

If you're so addicted to your device that you need to give it to your friend and sign a contract agreeing to pay her twenty dollars every time you ask for it back, with the additional stipulation that if she declines to hand it over when you ask and you protest, she can post whatever she wants on your Instagram and flick you thrice between the eyes, then you might want to just stay home and binge-watch baking shows on YouTube.

Web Sight

If you've planned well, you won't need to be online constantly to do things like research nearby attractions. Still, you never know when you might need to check the details of a reservation or call home in an emergency.

Used thoughtfully (that is, as a tool you consult with rather than a vortex you're absorbed into), the internet can take the sting out of would-be stressful moments. Last-minute itinerary adjustments. Driving directions. Even responding to your boss's urgent email. Those are the instances when technology shines. And since you don't know when they'll happen when you're traveling, your preference will probably be to maintain a wireless connection at all times. Here's how to do that.

SIM CITY

Tracking down a SIM card from a local provider when you arrive at your destination can be as simple as ordering pad thai on Uber

Eats or as onerous as tracking leopards on the Masai Mara. If you're lucky, there'll be a store at the airport that sells them. If you're unlucky, you'll be pantomiming with construction workers in the port of Athens to locate the nearest Vodafone store.

You'll have to first call your domestic service provider to make sure your phone is unlocked and capable of accepting foreign SIM cards. Any set of instructions whose first step is to call a 1-800 number is a set of instructions I'm ashamed to assign.

You can order a SIM card in advance—some savvy travelers get them delivered to their hotel—and set it up to activate on the day you arrive. This method requires that you retain the infinitesimal ejector pin to pop your current card out, not to mention the card itself, once popped. Taping it to a postcard and mailing it home to yourself seems like a more reliable plan, but maybe you're better than I am at keeping track of an object the size of a fingernail clipping.

Getting a foreign SIM card is not a good idea if you're intending to travel to multiple countries on the same trip. You would need a new one for every border you crossed.

If you insist on the foreign SIM card strategy, at least opt for one with unlimited data. The last thing you want to do is head *back* to the Vodafone store to request another 4 GB of data. That's a leopard you don't want to find.

SOME LIKE IT HOTSPOT

Next up on the list of functional but suboptimal internet solutions are portable Wi-Fi hotspots. These pucks give you LTE data abroad, but their value propositions are questionable.

The **Skyroam Solis Lite** is one of the best available hotspots for international travelers. The device itself costs $119.19. Then you can buy Wi-Fi access for up to ten devices by the gigabyte (GB) ($6), day ($9), or month ($99). Paying by the GB is a lousy value. You'll burn through it like the sun penetrating a Mediterranean mist. Unlimited data is the way to go.

Skyroam provides coverage in most, but not all, countries. Make sure to check that you'll be covered at your destination.

But if you're going to pay $9 per day for unlimited LTE data, do you really want a separate device? Probably not...

WHEN IN ROAM

And now, my favorite option. I call it the Do Nothing plan. Well, almost nothing.

Phone service providers know how desperate their customers are for internet access around the clock and around the world, and many of them offer reasonable international plans.

AT&T's International Day Pass, for example, is perfect for a 9-Day Getaway. It lets you use your domestic data plan abroad for $10 per day. **Verizon's TravelPass**, **Sprint's Global Roaming**, and **T-Mobile's international plans** offer similar services to reduce or eliminate roaming costs. Assuming you have an unlimited data plan, this defeats the purpose of a mobile hotspot.

Just remember to activate the plan before you depart. Doing entirely nothing is a surefire way to rack up exorbitant roaming charges. You might not see the harm in sending a quick text home. In the background, your entire email inbox will download, and you'll get slapped with a $450 bill for all the data you unwittingly used.

AT&T also has a monthly **Passport plan**, but the day plan is preferable. It works in twenty-four-hour increments, so you can potentially save money by keeping your phone in airplane mode for periodic detoxes.

Check the terms carefully on these plans as some tack on

additional fees or slower speeds after you've reached certain data thresholds. Terms also vary widely for talk and text.

Like checking to see if your phone accepts foreign SIM cards, this international data plan option might also require a call to your service provider. If that's the case, Godspeed. But in terms of overall convenience, almost nothing beats doing almost nothing.

SAVE THE DATA

If you're using anything besides an unlimited data plan, employ the following tactics to conserve data:

- On an iPhone, try "Low Data Mode" under Cellular Data Options, or turn off cellular data for specific apps.
- Under General, turn off "Background App Refresh."
- Turn off automatic app updates in the Play Store or App Store.
- Most social media apps have options to stop preloading or autoplaying video. YouTube has a toggle to play HD video on Wi-Fi only, and Netflix lets you set your default streaming quality on cellular.

But maybe instead of Netflix and chilling, you can chill with the Netflix. I hope you didn't go to Sweden to binge-watch *House of Cards*.

RAISE THE BARS

If your goal is not to pay a dime for internet access, you can get by just fine in most places. Sporadic connectivity could be a bugaboo for businesspeople who need to approve deals on DocuSign or Zoomers who would sooner starve than go forty-eight hours without joining a dance challenge on TikTok. If you can survive with here-and-there access, here are a few ways to track down full bars:

- Book a hotel with free Wi-Fi. Many that don't have great Wi-Fi in rooms still have central areas with stronger signals.
- Download the **Wi-Fi Finder + Map** app to locate public hotspots.
- Go where backpackers go, like that one bagel place in Prague where I once ate back-to-back-to-back-to-back asiago bagel sandwiches just so I could Google "What was Kafka's problem?" and try to post something on Facebook that would impress people I didn't even like.
- If you want to access the internet with your laptop and lack a Wi-Fi connection but have service on your phone, you can use your phone as a hotspot.
- Cafés and shops often have free Wi-Fi. Look for the hand-written chalk placard under the register.

PRIVATE EYES

One day, in my safe and cozy home where no bad guys ever come, I noticed an unusual Wi-Fi network amid the usual drop-down of all my neighbors' networks: "FBI Van."

One of my neighbors thought they were being clever. Good one, dweeb.

Then I looked outside and there was a shady van that I had never seen before parked directly outside my house. It was totally opaque and exactly what I've always imagined FBI vans to look like.

I have nothing to hide, so I wasn't worried, just a bit unsettled. Why were the Feds snooping around my block?

Then it occurred to me: what kind of weak-ass FBI van network name is "FBI Van" anyway? If you were the Feds, wouldn't you choose something that blended in more, like "CenturyLink2614-5G"? Would your network even appear?

The incident gave me the heebie-jeebies, and I immediately purchased a VPN.

A **VPN, or Virtual Private Network,** is a direct encrypted connection or private tunnel to the internet. Most websites that require a password have encryption built in, so a VPN, although advisable for protecting your personal data and sensitive information, is not necessary.

Ever since my encounter with the not-actual Feds, I use **Nord VPN** on all of my devices. You may, like me, not have anything to hide, but that doesn't negate the legions of hackers, faux federal agents, and worldwide weirdos probably prowling on undiscerning internet users in every airport and on every public network you've ever connected to. If you're the kind of person who gets paranoid about those kinds of creepers, play it safe and encrypt yourself.

Lost and Found

You went through all that trouble to get safe and reliable internet access. What are you going to do with it? Instead of mimicking all of your browsing and streaming habits from home, use practical apps that temper the disorientation you may be feeling.

Despite your heroic efforts to stay connected, many beneficial apps function seamlessly in their offline versions. In their data-devouring or downloaded forms, two clutch tools solve the pressing problems of foreign communication and navigation.

PLAIN LANGUAGE

Sure, you could try to become fluent in Swahili on DuoLingo two weeks before your trip to Uganda. Just promise me you won't spend so much time studying irregular verbs that you forget to learn basic phrases. Hello. Goodbye. Please. Thank you. Excuse me. Yes. No. How much? Bathroom. Not spicy. Too spicy. Help.

Have some fun with the camera feature on **Google Translate** to decipher menus and intimidating signs. Facilitate bilingual banter with the conversation feature. Pick up the pieces of your blown mind.

Although you can download languages on the app for offline use and tell Siri to speak Russian for you in a South African male accent, nothing beats a sincere effort to speak the native language with locals. Like a voicemail you leave for a friend on their birthday, it's endearing even if you butcher it.

ALL OVER THE MAP

Google for flight searching. Google for translation. Google for navigation. It's a fact: Google is really good at this stuff.

To download **Google Maps** for offline use, just search for a place and tap Download. You'll be able to zoom in or out and download a custom chunk of map that will be accessible even when you don't have service.

Be warned: these downloaded maps drink data. If you were about to pay for an international data plan simply to access maps, think again. The download method may save you the expense. When you need a map most, you probably won't have service anyway.

If you're the type of person who prefers to print all of your reservation confirmations, you might also prefer paper maps. I don't use them, but if I did, it would be for countries rather than cities and big-picture planning rather than in-transit GPS. Perhaps a paper map could also be a useful backup if Google Maps tries to tell you that the fastest route to your destination requires off-roading through a farm.

RITE OF DRAKE PASSAGE

If you thought finding fast internet in Europe was hard, good luck tracking down full bars in Antarctica.

There was Wi-Fi on the *National Geographic Explorer*, but it was as spotty as you'd expect and cost about a buck per minute. I didn't venture to Antarctica with my dad to go online. The choppy signal was the least of our concerns. It was the choppy water we were worried about.

The *Explorer* is one of the most advanced expedition vessels on earth. It is at once an ice-breaking megaship and a five-star hotel, equipped with state-of-the-art underwater cameras, a fleet of motorized Zodiacs, a fitness center, and spa. But it still struggles to navigate its biggest threat—the Drake Passage.

This notorious stretch of water, where two oceans collide at the tip of South America, can run the gamut from the "Drake Lake"—smooth as glass—to the "Drake Shake"—thirty-foot swells straight out of Ernest Shackleton's worst nightmare.

We hoped for the best and prepared for the wrath.

Our seasickness kit was a small pharmacy, including a full spectrum of preventative measures ranging in potency from ginger chews to Dramamine to the infamous Scopolamine patch. Everyone aboard the *Explorer* had Scopolamine on deck. It's a sticker you put on the soft spot behind your ear.

I didn't know what the patch would do to me besides quell my nausea, but I felt comforted knowing I had a last line of defense, if it came to that. The patch needs a twenty-four-hour head start to be effective. We checked the daily weather report with dread, trying to gauge how treacherous the next day's ride would be. It didn't matter. We would have to endure whatever Mother Nature threw at us.

On the outbound journey from Ushuaia to the Antarctic Peninsula, which takes two full days, we were blessed with a silky sailing across the Drake. It might as well have been Lake Washington. I popped half a Bonine and ate twelve ginger chews.

It was early February, midsummer, cold but not frigid. Occasionally, on our daily Zodiac excursions, the sky turned dark and the wind whipped across the ice. Despite wearing five layers, it was so cold that I felt like I was standing in the middle of a blizzard in my underwear. Every freezing gust reminded me that the return trip across the Drake still lay in front of us.

The day before our return voyage to Ushuaia, the captain came on the ship-wide intercom system to warn us, "If you've still got your patches, you might want to put them on tonight. We may be in for a bumpy ride."

Despite seismic, undulating, vertigo-inducing swells that rocked us simultaneously front to back and side to side; despite the ship being catapulted into the sky only to slam down into the depths of a gaping oceanic crater just as another wave came crashing, shooting walls of violent white water over the edge of the bow; despite the anguish of my inner ears, I did not get seasick. The patch worked.

But I did go semi-blind. My throat burned like I'd swallowed fire. I felt so groggy that even if I could have seen, I couldn't have stood. My stomach, however, was as calm as a placid sea.

Somehow, amid all the Drake Passage hullabaloo, no one bothered to warn us of Scopolamine's side effects. To perform its chief duty, the medicine ravages most other bodily faculties, inducing a host of malaises ranging from brain fog to skin rash. Lying face-down on my twin bed, feeling as blended as frozen berries, I wondered if perhaps not applying the patch would have been a better course of action.

Meanwhile, my dad was struggling in his own way. Our cabin was equipped with a small desk, which we used as our charging station. We tried to keep the cords and batteries tidy, but as the only countertop in the room, the desk was constantly cluttered with ginger, gloves, sunscreen, and small plates of cake and brownies we'd pilfered from the dining room. Whenever either of us wanted to upload photos on our computers, we pushed all the electronics and desserts on the desk aside, creating just enough space for our laptop. Unfortunately, when you're crossing the Drake Passage in a polar tsunami, "just enough" still isn't enough.

The ship had made one dangerous cabin oversight. Not only was the desk glass, but it slid out, leaving space underneath to spread out a map. It was a mariner's workstation, a cartographer's delight. We certainly didn't need an app to cram cookies in it.

In the maw of the Drake, out of boredom, my dad decided to organize photos on his hard drive. Whenever the water mellowed out enough for the contents of the desk to stop sliding, he hunched over his computer to drag and drop a batch of jpegs. Inevitably, within minutes, a colossal wave would crack against the hull, tipping his chair as he grasped for handrails.

I hardly knew what planet I was on, and my eyes felt like I'd worn the same pair of contacts for three straight weeks, so I couldn't muster the strength to help him or even offer to. His noble but failed spells of attempted "work" continued in lightning-like episodes, with each subsequent crash sending lenses, caps, cards, cords, sunglasses, slices of pie, and all remaining expedition bijouterie cascading into my dad's lap, followed by the glass plank, bounced at last out of its groove. It slammed into his abdomen like an accidentally unlocked tray table. He mumbled curses as I chuckled at his plight, urging him to give up and lie down. Finally, he surrendered to The Shake, sweeping everything that wasn't yet on the floor onto it in that melodramatic way movie characters clear tables to show how mad they are.

For the next full day, we lay there, wheezing and praying, with thousands of dollars' worth of camera gear thrashing all over the carpet. We only got up to pee or, I should say, down to pee, since we resorted to crawling over the glass desktop which now blocked the bathroom door like a sheet of ice we had no choice but to traverse.

The bathroom door weighed a ton and wouldn't stay open. If we took our hand off it for a second, it contused us. Compared to the dim cabin lighting, the bathroom light was a blinding strobe, but because I was already blind, it merely induced a migraine. I bounced back to bed, flopping off the walls like one of those giant inflatable humanoids at a used car dealership.

Collapsing onto my side, I caught a glimpse of the horizon. It was vertical. I kid you not, the entire ocean had been knocked off its axis. I celebrated this surreal moment by chewing another quarter pound of ginger and punching in for some quality Wi-Fi time. When I woke up three hours later, the page was still loading.

No matter what you spend or sacrifice to stay plugged in on your voyage, sometimes the best way to connect is to pull the plug. Surrender to the elements. Ask your travel companion for antihistamines. Ask a stranger for directions. Put your phone away. Shackleton survived hunger and frostbite. My dad and I escaped the Drake. You'll be fine.

CHAPTER 16

Commit to Memories

"I have a secret treasure upon which I can draw at will. I can bring forth, on the darkest day, bright diamonds of remembered joys, diamonds whose many facets reflect some happy dream come true, a small ambition gratified, a long-sought sensation, caught and savored to the full."

—BURTON HOLMES

WHEN I WAS seventeen, I traveled to Chile with a cultural immersion program for high school students. While there, I took hundreds of photos in the mystical Atacama, land of Mars rover testing, UFO observation, and awesome dunes. My love of travel photography solidified.

Flying home, airport security found and threatened to confiscate a lapis lazuli letter opener in my backpack. It was a gift, and I refused to part with it. I'd already checked my suitcase. In a fit of impatience and naïveté, I checked my backpack, too.

Thankfully, when I claimed the bag in Seattle, the letter opener was still there, but my camera and all my photos were gone.

Why I ever thought checking my camera in an unlocked back-pack was a good idea is beyond me. I have been obsessively taking, organizing, editing, saving, and resaving my travel photos ever since.

Losing digital travel records hurts so badly because visual documentation bolsters memory. Photography has the power to pull you into a moment, heighten your attention, and make you profoundly appreciate a scene.

But you can only tap into that higher state of awareness when you aim to capture the authentic essence of a moment rather than being overly focused on manipulating its presentation to be more impressive, Instagramable, or staged. Done right, the process of documenting your trip intensifies your enjoyment of it. Obsessive attachment to the eventual sharing of that documentation only hinders your enjoyment.

Capture photos and footage on your getaway for yourself first. Use photographs, journals, and keepsakes to enhance your memories, not to replace them.

If you're going to document your experience, you might as well try to do it well. Back up your photos and remember, as far as airport security is concerned, a letter opener is a knife.

Photo Bombs

What's your definition of a good photo? Do you have to be in the photo for it to be good? Do you have to *not* be in it?

Think about your best travel photos from previous trips. What makes them special? Why do they stand out in your memory? A "good" photo isn't necessarily one that would win an award in a photography competition.

Many of my favorite travel photos are funny accidents or ironies. The great ones are evocative. They capture a feeling that the viewer can tap into. Even if the photo isn't technically perfect or impressive, it can still be good if it conveys a mood, communicates something about the subject or the photographer, or both.

If your definition of a good photo is one that gets the most likes on Instagram, fill as much of the frame as possible with your butt.

SEIZE THE MOMENT

There are three primary elements of an excellent travel photo: light, composition, and moment. Most travel photos have one or two of these elements. If two, usually the first two.

A sense of moment is the most elusive element, the element that makes a good photo exceptional and impossible to imitate. It's the element of timing, that serendipitous, there-it-was-and-now-it's-gone dimension. If I went to the same spot where you took your photo, and the light was nearly identical, and I copied your composition exactly, I still couldn't duplicate your photo because the moment has passed.

When I visited the Christ the Redeemer statue in Rio de Janeiro, the fog was so dense that the statue was invisible even while standing directly underneath it. A crowd of tourists waited for the haze to lift and Christ to reveal himself. When it happened, everyone lifted their camera in unison. I turned around and took a photo of the crowd, worshipping Jesus with their lenses. I may not have the cleanest snap of the statue, but I made an image that captured my experience, at that moment, most accurately.

STORY TIME

When I photograph travel stories for magazines, editors request and expect an assortment of images that collectively tell a story.

A typical travel story combines a sweeping vista or establishing shot to set the scene, an image of a person or people, a food or architecture shot, and at least one detail shot. If you return from a trip with a camera full of landscapes or photos of every meal or beverage you consumed, you wouldn't have a story.

To convey the diversity, color, and rhythm of a place, you need a mix of images that not only puts the place in geographical and historical context but also conveys its cultural nuances and sensory undertones.

Try to create a photographic mosaic of your trip as if your story were going to be featured in a magazine. Consider creating a shot list to gamify the process. Don't worry so much about making technically perfect photos. Focus on the interplay among them. Capture pieces of the place so you can reassemble the puzzle at home.

PAINT A PORTRAIT

Flipping through the glossy pages of *National Geographic Traveler*, I froze on a striking image. The photographer, Catherine Karnow, took it at a decadent restaurant in Mallorca. It has a pillared patio adorned with ferns and flowers and oversized candles on each table, all lit during daytime. The walls are painted with a faded fresco, and matching statues of goddesses and cherubs compete for space on a Babylonian terrace dripping with exotic bouquets.

The restaurant is full of sophisticated patrons, but in the foreground of the frame, a young Omar Sharif look-alike steals the viewer's attention. Karnow caught him gesticulating with arms open and hands spread. A semi-blurred waiter whisking away a tray of drinks conveys a sense of action, and a distant city adds mystery to the festive scene. It's a perfect environmental portrait.

Try taking a similar portrait to Karnow's of a dynamic person in their natural habitat. A wide lens is your safest bet to capture the setting and subject in one. If it feels intimidating, creepy, or rude to photograph a stranger without them noticing, use your environmental portrait goal as a reason to strike up a conversation with a photogenic local. They'll be more comfortable posing for you if you take a genuine interest in them. The photo you take will be better, too.

National Geographic photos are remarkably intimate. Those photographers sometimes spend weeks or months with the same group of people until their subjects seem to forget there's a photographer present.

Travel photography has been cannibalized to mean "photography while traveling," which defaults to vainglorious, cliché poses in front of monuments whose meaning is never learned. At least once on your trip, go full NatGeo. Be patient, frame the shot, and wait for your Omar Sharif doppelgänger to showcase his bravado. It will be worth it.

RESPECT YOUR SELFIE

I once saw an elderly tourist in Melbourne using a selfie stick, except she wasn't using it to take a selfie. The camera was facing outward. She wasn't reaching the stick way out to the side or above her head to achieve an otherwise unreachable vantage point. She just really wanted to use a selfie stick. Bless her heart!

I take selfies and have nothing against them. If taking a selfie makes you happy and you're not encroaching on anyone else's safety, fun, or peace, then by all means, snap away.

In my experience, the best instance to take a selfie is when there's no one else around, however adept behind a lens, to ask, "Would you mind taking a photo of us?"

The selfie I took of me and my dad in a kayak in Antarctica.

The selfie I took in Iceland's Blue Lagoon, when I visited solo and brought my camera into the cloudy, cerulean water, holding it with both hands like a porcelain vase.

The selfie I took with my compatriots Josh and Colin in the front row at the USA's opening World Cup match in Natal, Brazil.

To have captured those moments substantiated the foolish feeling of procurement through selfie-ing.

Instead of the traditional extended-arm or selfie-stick selfie, I much prefer and recommend the tripod/self-timer selfie. It's more of a self-portrait. No awkward arms or sticks involved.

I travel with a small, bendy tripod, the **Joby GorillaPod**. It always comes in handy, even if I use it only once per trip, in the perfect spot at golden hour when all the other tourists have cleared out of the frame.

If you ever forgo a selfie and ask a stranger to take your picture, choose wisely who you ask and make sure your camera is on Auto mode to make their job as easy as possible.

BACKUP PLAN

If you don't care about capturing or preserving remarkable travel photos and just want to snap some iPhone quickies, feel free to ignore this section.

But if you intend to make images worth protecting, protect them well. Backing up photos means making duplicates of the original files, in their original sizes and file types, on a separate device.

Do you need to bring your laptop on your trip to accomplish this? I wish I could give you a hard no, but it's the best solution for serious photographers. Bring an SD card reader and an external hard drive. Use your laptop to move files from the card to the drive. Done.

I bring my laptop on trips as well as two external hard drives, both **LaCie Rugged** drives (try the **Seagate Backup Plus Slim** for less bulk). Every night, I move my photos to both drives. Now my photos are in three places. They're on the hard drives and they're still on the SD card. I'll throw them on the cloud, too, if I can. (I told you that Chile catastrophe cut me deep.)

Never clear your SD cards on the road. Wait until you get home to delete photos. One accident can be devastating. The transfer didn't work, but you already cleared the card. You deleted the wrong photos. The goal is to make the original photos redundant, not to destroy them.

If you have a camera with built-in Wi-Fi, you can transfer photos to your device wirelessly. If you have an iPhone or iPad, you can buy a Lightning to SD Card dongle. Both methods gobble up storage space and can be slow. Plus, you may only be able to transfer JPG files and not movies or RAW files.

Selectively transferring photos to your device over Wi-Fi is a smart way to conserve space. Got some winners? At least transfer the images you'd be devastated to lose, like that gem you just snapped of your iced vanilla latte.

Bring enough SD cards that you don't have to worry about filling them up, or get a few higher-capacity (128 GB) cards. Guard these tiny plastic chips containing nothing less than all of your most precious memories carefully, and that includes handling them while switching them out.

I was once snapping away at an ancient fortress, ran out of space on my SD card, and had to make an unsecured swap. But right as I was making the switch from full to fresh card—I can't make this stuff up—I got attacked by a cluster of fire ants. They ransacked my ankles and shins. I did what anyone getting attacked by fire ants would do: a spasmodic, keeled-over rendition of the Macarena. As I frantically brushed the fire brigade off my calves, I dropped the full card. It taunted me with too many bounces on the cobblestones before disappearing into the drain beneath me.

Trauma—we learn from it. Note that carrying multiple SD cards doesn't count as backing up.

Your final option is a wireless hard drive with a built-in SD card reader, like the shockproof **GnarBox 2.0**, but those tend to be pricey. By now, you've almost come full circle back to laptop land. You might as well get a cheap **ASUS** machine or borrow a friend's 2012 MacBook Air with a fan that sounds like a tornado.

Who Writes This Stuff?

You gaze out the train window and then down at the blank, open notebook in your lap. You sit in silence with the truth of your displacement, amid a penetrating foreignness. You are who you've always been, yet everything feels new.

A blank journal page is just as intimidating as a blank document on a computer screen, with your cursor flashing to the cadence of your heartbeat.

William Zinsser, author of the timeless writing guide *On Writing Well*, explains in an essay called "Why I Travel" that he writes "to validate my experience…The act of writing organizes how I spend my time when I arrive in a place. It gives me information, concentrates my thoughts, and opens doors I wouldn't otherwise be allowed to knock on."

Think of journaling as mental photography. Even throwaway photos in your camera roll trigger memories, stories, and emotions. Likewise, even writing down a short list of what you recently saw and did could trigger a revelation when the trip is over.

If you despise writing, try sketching. Either way, if you're so inclined, get yourself a high-quality hardback notebook or sketchbook from **Leuchtturm1917**. Quality stationery turns mundane journaling into a noble exercise.

Need ideas to fill an empty page? Try these prompts:

- Why did I decide to come here?
- How is this place different from what I expected? What do I see now that I didn't see before?
- So much about home seems so much clearer now that I'm away. For example…
- The most absurd/awesome/notable person or experience I witnessed, interacted with, or took part in recently is…
- What's the most honest thing I feel right now, without a trace of sarcasm or self-consciousness?
- The best-case scenario after I finish writing this is…
- I deserve an Oscar for the performance I put on when…In my acceptance speech, I would definitely have to thank…
- If I could bottle up this moment, it would taste/smell/look/sound/feel like…
- One seemingly inconsequential thing I saw today that made a lasting impression on me is…
- I feel nervous about…But I know everything is going to be fine because…
- A year from now, this trip will be…And I will be…

AHA MEMENTO

In college, I was on a bowling team with three buddies. There was an unspoken tradition in our league that whenever an errant pin flung out into the gutter, beyond the reach of the rake board, the bowler had to scurry down the side of the lane, grab the pin, hide it in their jacket, and take it home. It was a sophomoric tradition, but I partook, and still have my pin to this day. I considered getting rid of it. What good is a bowling pin anyway? But a few years after college, one of my three bowling teammates tragically died of brain cancer. My pilfered pin took on a new significance.

On the Greek island of Symi, I met an Italian shopkeeper with an electric personality. His name was Jacopo. He sold exotic jewelry, textiles, and home decor, sourced from his extensive travels in Central Asia. While in the shop, he regaled me, almost entirely with his hands, with stories of his escapades around the world, weaving in hilarious impersonations and descriptions of various nationalities. The time in London when he tripped and fell into the Thames, then was offered soup because "they love their soup." The Estonians he met in bleak Tallinn and their evident hatred for Russians (insert curmudgeonly Italian-tinged Estonian growl here). Canadians? "The wind blows right through them." (I wonder what he says about Americans when Canadians roll through his shop.) Let's not forget the disturbing incident in Tulum when he stumbled into a psychedelic retreat and witnessed tripping tourists licking the glands of hallucinogenic Sonoran toads (it's a thing). I could have spent the whole day listening to Jacopo's off-the-cuff stand-up routine and rubbing every silk *suzani* in his shop.

I left with a pair of ikat *friulane* (more slippers). But it wasn't the shoes alone I took home with me; it was the memory of that interaction, of stylish Symi and its worldly transplants, the joy of making fast friends with a stranger. The slippers are proxies for the kinds of surprises only discovered in neoclassical dreamscapes.

Souvenirs don't necessarily have to document your trip. If you truly love something, that alone is reason enough to take it home. Just make sure the procurement of the souvenir is organic, not forced. Although the object will always be associated with its place of origin, ideally its discovery would be spontaneous, a pleasant happenstance that becomes linked with a place and a memory. Never buy a souvenir simply as evidence that you were somewhere.

A souvenir shop is the worst place to buy a souvenir, unless you're in the market for magnets, T-shirts, snow globes, mugs, baseball hats, keychains, and flimsy canvas bags. There's nothing mindful about a tchotchke. If it's mass-produced, it's a lousy souvenir, in my not-so-humble opinion.

The best souvenirs are things you were already in want and need of. If you need sandals or a certain decor item for your living room and stumble upon the perfect pair or piece, that's a win.

Scented or edible products evoke strong memories and thus allow the trip to linger in your immediate memory a bit longer. As consumables, they are fleeting and must be savored.

On the side of a craggy road in Crete, carved into a cliffside dotted with bee boxes, Annie and I stumbled upon a man at a wood stand with a sign that read "Cretan Traditional Products." He had thyme-infused honey, herbs, and ointments. We bought a few jars of a chamomile, calendula, olive oil, and beeswax balm. It was the most heavenly all-purpose ointment I've ever used, and although it, like the trip, eventually depleted, using it soothed the sting of not being in the southern Aegean.

If you buy nonconsumable goods that you intend to display, you should know exactly where they'll go in your home. If you buy clothing, you should know exactly how and when you'll wear the item. Make sure the piece translates to your home environment. Please don't be the nincompoop who comes back from Puerto Vallarta with a giant sombrero.

My favorite souvenirs are free. Annie and I have some beautiful rocks and shells from our travels together around the world. The individual pieces don't hold any extraordinary value, but as a whole, the assortment reminds us of all the places we've been together.

I wish I could say my Aquafina bottle filled with Ganges River water from Varanasi, India is my most prized souvenir. As pleased as I am with the wherewithal demonstrated to lower my plastic goblet into that holy current, I'm kind of afraid of it. A fascinatingly grotesque clump of multicolored biogas has been festering at the base of the bottle for over a decade now. The bottle itself is warped to the brink of implosion, and the experiment probably belongs in a dumpster. I keep it in my childhood bedroom despite having long since cleared out all of my possessions from the space. I just want a place to not have to look at my Ganges water or make a final decision to toss it. And that confession is proof enough that not all "natural" souvenirs are worth claiming, especially not the ones you end up banishing to the attic or storage locker.

Collections are fun but dangerous. It starts innocently enough with hotel keys, salt and pepper shakers, or pins. Next thing you know, you have an entire closet in your house devoted to your dagger collection. Here's the Berber *koummya* from Morocco, and here's the double-edged Maasai *seme* from Kenya, oh but let's not forget the Toledan *falcata* from Spain. You know, I could really use someplace to store my Dyson vacuum cleaner, but hey, you never know when you'll need a blunt *bolo* sheathed in dung-scented kudu hide, am I right?

Gifts from Above

No one needs a souvenir from a trip they didn't take.

The purpose of a gift you give someone from your travels is to be a token of the fact that you were thinking of them when you were gone.

Many of the same guiding questions that apply to buying souvenirs for yourself also apply to gifts.

Will the item be equally appreciable in its new home as it was in its land of origin? Will the hand-embroidered Mexican blouse you bought your friend in Oaxaca really fit into her wardrobe in Michigan?

Will it have the same significance to someone who lacks the emotional tie to the place?

Is it high quality? Or is it, upon closer inspection, a piece of shiitake mushroom?

Are you forcing it? Don't set out with a shopping list in your head. Wait to find gems organically.

Remember that you're not obligated to get your friends and family gifts, and they're not obligated to keep any gift you give them. If and when you do give a gift, remind the recipient of that non-obligation. Tell them, "If this means nothing to you, feel free to toss it. I won't be offended." Mean it.

It's okay to ruin the surprise. You could tell your mother before you depart, "Hey, Mom, I'm going to a famous candle store in Istanbul. I know you love the aromas of sandalwood, vanilla, and vetiver. If I found something with those scents, is that something you might be interested in?"

Her reaction to that will tell you everything you need to know.

CHAPTER 16

Memory Banking

Memories are the consolation prizes for the fleetingness of life and travel. They remain with us long after the moments that inspire them elapse. Synthesized in our minds, our memories become integral parts of us.

The records you keep, whether digital or physical, should serve as bridges between experience and memory. They should prolong and crystallize the experience, so much so that in time, the artifacts themselves become superfluous.

Once the memories are locked in, go forward into the next nirvana.

CHAPTER 17

Homecoming

"We shall not cease from exploration
And the end of all our exploring
Will be to arrive where we started
And know the place for the first time."
—T. S. ELIOT

WHENEVER MY MOM returns from a trip, she says, "It's good to be home."

Sometimes, she says it even when it's not good. After trips we've taken together, in the taxi home from the airport, she'll say it, and I'll think to myself, "It is?"

Coming home can be even more intimidating than leaving, especially if you neglected to prepare for your return before you left. (Return to Chapter 9 to avoid this scenario.)

Astronauts have been known to fall into depression when they return from space. Who can blame Buzz Aldrin for his post-lunar funk? After experiencing something so rare, home seems hollow at first.

It hasn't changed. You have. You've learned how to see the world through the lens of wonder. Now you must turn that lens on everything that appears dull, until the ordinary becomes extraordinary.

After a few minutes, hours, or days, being home gets good, if for no other reason than sleeping in your own bed again.

Home is familiar, comfortable, nurturing, and sacred. Get excited about the life you've returned to. If your trip lit you up, shine that light on routine habits and practices. Unwrap the gifts you didn't even know you brought home. The rhythms and rituals. The matcha ceremony. The handmade pasta technique. The fearless fashion. The slow meal. The simple joy of walking.

Besides, if you choose to see the end of one trip as the beginning of another, you have nothing to mope about. You'll get away again soon enough.

In the meantime, stick the landing. Finish your trip with the same sense of purpose that guided you all along.

Start pretending you're on the ground while you're still in the sky. What's for dinner when you land? Should you order Uber Eats the moment you hit the runway to save yourself the agony of a late-night empty refrigerator? Signs point to yes. Better yet, order a grocery delivery from the plane. It will be worth the price of in-flight Wi-Fi.

Crank up your Nest thermostat from your phone to give it a head start. Call your doggie daycare or snake sitter. Tell them you're coming to get your baby.

Don't think I've forgotten about all of your crap…

A Lot to Unpack

I mentioned earlier in this book that Annie taught me how to pack. She also taught me how to unpack. And for a while, I hated her for it. That's because, according to her method, unpacking happens the moment you get home.

Don't even sit down. An object in motion stays in motion. Unpacking gets exponentially less desirable with every passing moment after opening your front door. Waiting to unpack will never make it feel less like a chore. It's like doing the dishes. It's never fun. But it's even worse to do today's dishes tomorrow or next week.

I used to half-unpack in the initial hours after returning home, emptying my backpack into a corner of my office, then getting distracted by a mound of mail. I'll deal with my backpack tomorrow, I'd tell myself.

That would go on for a week or so, until the piles became invisible. In the meantime, I didn't know where anything was. Dirty socks I hid in zippered pockets grew mildew, and whatever remaining motivation I had to finish the job waned. While I was stuck in unpacking purgatory, Annie would be fully unpacked before her head hit the pillow. The discrepancy in tactics was impossible to ignore, and in time, I became a convert.

If you pack well and keep your bag organized, unpacking is not arduous. First, deposit dirty laundry into your hamper and throw a first load in. Next, put your cosmetics back in their rightful locations in the bathroom. Put your tech gear away—all the way away. Then put your suitcase away. To quote the simplicity queen, "Don't even think about putting your filthy suitcase on your bed, you absolute unhinged barbarian."

You're bound to have traveled with things you'll need to bring back into immediate use, like underwear. Also, it's nine days' worth of stuff. It's not that much.

If you can't unpack fully, at least take the pouches to their rooms, and do as much of the preliminary work as possible. At the bare minimum, get your suitcase out of sight.

Nobody Cares

"How was your trip?" they ask. You can hardly formulate an answer.

How do you convey to others, in a concise and non-boring way, why your trip was so transformative?

The question is so difficult to answer because most people don't ask themselves the same question before they try to answer it.

This final reflection is the most crucial, but most neglected, piece of the travel equation. The point of travel is expansion, and growth comes through thoughtful responses to questions such as:

- What did I learn about myself?
- What new values or ideas did I take away?
- How am I going to implement those values and ideas into my everyday life?
- How am I going to give to others more fully with the additional knowledge or insight I've gained?

How was Japan? Stunning. It showed me how excellence is achieved through practice and precision, and if I can be more attentive to detail, I can elevate my art and anything else I choose to pursue.

How was Greece? Heavenly. I keep going back because it reminds me that "the good life" lies in the small, everyday moments with friends, family, and food that's made and eaten with care.

How was Antarctica? No words. The combination of beauty and terror in those icebergs made me think about how random and fleeting our time on earth is, and in that context, I'm less hesitant to take risks and less afraid to fail.

Having a clear takeaway is significant not because it makes you more interesting at dinner parties (though you will be) but because of the perspective it solidifies in you.

If you're the kind of person who likes or is often called upon to give recap presentations of your adventures, consider what would make watching someone else's trip recap entertaining for you. You'd want the trip to come to life. You'd want to feel like you were there. You'd want to hear only the traveler's best and most succinct stories. You'd want a reason to care.

Despite your best efforts to make others care, they still probably won't. Be okay with that.

Afterglow

The hedonic benefit of a trip fades quickly upon return. Although no one likes a boring slideshow, sharing stories of your getaway with others is the most foolproof way to safeguard and compound your satisfaction.

As discussed in Chapter 2, the chief advantage experiences have over material goods is that they're more fun to talk about and more socially acceptable, too. Shared experiences yield greater connection and kinship. They're bigger parts of our identities than material possessions are.

Savoring a getaway through positive reminiscence ensures that the happiness you felt in the lead-up to your trip, and while taking it, doesn't disappear when the trip ends. Researchers who studied the happiness of 225 tourists in South Korea found that a travel-induced spike in overall life satisfaction lasted for, on average, one month after participants returned home.

One month isn't bad, but how can we prolong that time frame?

By harnessing memories rather than memorabilia and reminiscing frequently.

Your mind already has a tendency for rosy retrospection, a habit of transmuting events, even negative ones, into positive memories. The more you talk about your trip, the rosier your retrospection will become.

Perhaps your trip reminded you that there's more to life than work, or that people or cultures you thought were different really aren't that different at all. Perhaps it showed you how capable you are of overcoming challenges or revealed to you how much you had been taking for granted.

Your trip transcends circumstance when you glean and integrate valuable lessons from it. Telling people how your trip transformed you is a good start. *Being* transformed is the end goal.

No trip I've ever taken has been perfect. Every itinerary could have been tweaked or amended. It happens. That's why we all must keep traveling.

Tell your stories, retell them, and bask in the afterglow of nine days you'll never forget.

CONCLUSION

Four people in a Mercedes-Benz on a winding cliff-top road in Santorini. One driver. One photographer. One bride. One groom.

We were on our elopement photoshoot, darting from Oia to Imerovigli. The distance between villages is short, but hiring a car was the right move, and one of my favorite memories from my wedding came in it.

Our driver and photographer had met only twenty minutes earlier. They conversed in Greek as we soaked in the view from the back seat, beaming and basking in our first hour as newlyweds. In predictably Greek fashion, they had become so friendly with each other in such a short period of time that one might have mistaken them for brothers.

They laughed uproariously together. Breathless guffaws filled the space between their joyful gasps. Our photographer slapped his knees as the driver rocked back and forth, cracking up while apparently imitating some hypothetical fool. We looped around hair-raising turns on Santorini's most unnerving stretch of road. I would have been concerned had the driver not handled each curve so adroitly. He could have driven that road with his eyes closed.

"What is it?" I finally shouted after waiting for a good moment to interject, even though I knew there wasn't one. "What's so funny?"

The driver didn't speak English. Our photographer spoke it fluently but had trouble translating the punchline that had elicited such ecstatic mirth.

He did his best to explain. They had been talking about the concept of "later" and how so many people—not Greeks, clearly—spent their whole lives worrying about the future. That was it. That was the punchline. It was the funniest concept they could have possibly imagined.

"People always talk about tomorrow. What about tomorrow? Maybe tomorrow!"

What was I missing? It was funny, but not *that* funny. Then the driver chimed in with the only three words of English he spoke all day.

"Not tomorrow, TODAY!"

The "today" rang like church bells in his thick Greek accent. It wasn't the curtailed, anglicized "t'day" but rather a symphony of echoing vowels: "Toudaeieh!"

There was divine wisdom in their unbridled glee. The real joke was the tragic folly of lesser mortals who, living under the tyranny of tomorrow, couldn't grasp the most fundamental truth of existence, a truth that, to the two men in the front seats of our wedding car, was as self-evident as the sun.

We spent the rest of the afternoon scampering over whitewashed chapels and releasing white balloons into the endless blue. All the while, our driver's jubilant words resounded in my head. I hear them every time my mind scurries off toward Tomorrowville, failing to savor the magic of the present moment.

What's the point of worrying about tomorrow when you're getting married right now? That's what planning a trip as meticulously as you'd plan a wedding—or, better yet, a trip that is also a wedding—does for you. It eases the burden of tomorrow.

A well-planned trip invites elation and precludes regret, putting tomorrow in its place and insisting that you show up to today's party.

When you're on a winding cliff-top road in Santorini, be there. When you're sweating in a taxi line, be there. Wherever you are, be exactly there, exactly then.

You designed it that way.

Reclaim Your Freedom

Life is so perfect I could drink it with two straws. But I'd rather share my second straw with you.

You deserve a getaway. You deserve the joy of looking forward and the delight of looking back. You deserve experiences worth savoring. The perfectly imperfect ones you generated with unwavering intention, the random ones when fate intervened, and the challenging ones you thought would break you but only emboldened you.

You deserve the satisfaction of turning a dream into a reality, and the chief reward of that crystallization: understanding your own capacity to generate any outcome or feeling you desire.

You owe it to yourself to stop believing in imagined dangers that inculcate you with the lie of "I can't." You can dispossess or destroy them as easily as you feed them with fear and doubt. All the proof you need lies in the seed of your vision for your ideal trip. Your imagination conjured that dream no differently than it conjured the list of reasons why it won't work or has to be hard. It doesn't.

Now you have the blueprint to execute your vision—to plan with purpose, expand time, and reclaim true freedom. If you're going to believe in any of your mind's whimsical inventions, believe in possibility. Believe in business class to Asia. Believe in cooking class in Italy. Believe in a new class of mindful travelers with the power to find purpose and achieve equilibrium in any environment or situation.

If you're still scared of leaving home behind, take it with you. Sprinkle it on a foreign place until that place feels more familiar. Bottle up some foreignness (or Ganges water) and bring it back to replenish the pieces of home you took away. Earth is your home, and you deserve to feel at home anywhere on it—when the waves are choppy, where the guards are gruff, and even if you're uncomfortable. You deserve freedom.

We are entering a travel renaissance. Soon, there will be autonomous hovercrafts and hydrogen-powered planes. We'll hop on hyperloops and feel like we've teleported. We'll move faster and easier through, across, and into the world than ever before. Office life and work culture will continue to evolve into a more flexible future. We'll look back at photos of our masked-up selves and smile, and be able to see each other's smiles, and smile bigger. Technology will catapult us into the golden age of convenience, yet only intensify our craving for connection. Travel is the antidote to fill the spiritual void.

You deserve a full life, one in which you see yourself as you are in the light that exploration shines on you. You deserve the weightlessness of expectations defied, friendships forged, and marvels beheld. You deserve to become a child again—a child with no tantrums to throw, only a head to throw back and arms to throw up in awe at the miracle of Otherwhere enveloping you.

I've shared my continental drift. You've felt my tectonic plates collide. Now it's your turn. Not tomorrow. Today.

Get Away!

Continue the conversation at davidaxelrod.co, where you'll find a suite of free worksheets and checklists to further simplify the trip planning process. Shop the official *Get Away!* store, join the *Get Away!* community, or get in touch with David at davidaxelrod.co/contact.

REFERENCES

"2018 Work and Well-Being Survey." *American Psychological Association.* http://www.apaexcellence.org/assets/general/2018-work-and -wellbeing-survey-results.pdf?_ga=2.160272190.244065508 .1625095433-110081794.1625095433.

"2019 Airline Water Study by CUNY's Hunter College NYC Food Policy Center." EurekAlert! August 29, 2019. https://www .eurekalert.org/pub_releases/2019-08/tcuo-2awo82919.php.

"2020 Luxury Travel Trends." Small Luxury Hotels of the World, January 21, 2020. https://latteluxurynews.com/wp-content/uploads /2020/02/slh-luxury-travel-trends-2020-final-compressed.pdf.

Achor, Shawn, and Michelle Gielan. 2016. "The Data-Driven Case for Vacation." *Harvard Business Review*, July 13, 2016. https://hbr.org /2016/07/the-data-driven-case-for-vacation.

Adler, Judith. 1989. "Travel as Performed Art." *American Journal of Sociology* 94, no. 6: 1366–91. http://www.jstor.org/stable/2780963.

Ali, Rafat. 2015. "Travel Habits of Americans: 42 Percent Didn't Take Any Vacation Days in 2014." Skift, January 5, 2015. https://skift.com /2015/01/05/travel-habits-of-americans-41-percent-didnt-take-any -vacation-days-in-2014/.

"American Vacation Deprivation Levels at a Five-Year High." Expedia. com, October 16, 2018. https://newsroom.expedia.com/2018-10-16 -American-vacation-deprivation-levels-at-a-five-year-high.

Aspinwall, Lisa G. 2011. "Future-Oriented Thinking, Proactive Coping, and the Management of Potential Threats to Health and Well-Being." In *The Oxford Handbook of Stress, Health, and Coping*, edited by S. Folkman, 334–65. New York: Oxford University Press.

https://www.oxfordhandbooks.com/view/10.1093/oxfordhb
/9780195375343.001.0001/oxfordhb-9780195375343-e-017.

Belkic, Karen L., Paul A. Landsbergis, Peter l. Schnall, and Dean
Baker. 2004. "Is Job Strain a Major Source of Cardiovascular Disease?" *Scandinavian Journal of Work and Environmental Health* 30:
85–128. https://pubmed.ncbi.nlm.nih.gov/15127782/.

Bhattacharjee, Amit, and Cassie Mogilner. 2014. "Happiness from
Ordinary and Extraordinary Experiences." *Journal of Consumer
Research* 41, no. 1: 1–17. https://academic.oup.com/jcr/article-abstract
/41/1/1/1810271?redirectedFrom=fulltext.

Blasche, Gerhard W., Anna Arlinghaus, and Thomas E. Dorner. 2014.
"Leisure Opportunities and Fatigue in Employees: A Large Cross-
Sectional Study." *Leisure Sciences* 36: 235–50. https://www.tand
fonline.com/doi/abs/10.1080/01490400.2014.886981.

Bryant, F. B., Colette M. Smart, and Scott P. King. 2005. "Using the
Past to Enhance the Present: Boosting Happiness through Positive
Reminiscence." *Journal of Happiness Studies* 6: 227–60. https://link
.springer.com/article/10.1007/s10902-005-3889-4.

Bryant, Fred B., and Joseph Veroff. 2007. *Savoring: A New Model of
Positive Experience.* Mahwah, NJ: Lawrence Erlbaum.

Burgess, Helen. 2011. "Using Bright Light and Melatonin to Reduce
Jet Lag." In *Behavioral Treatments for Sleep Disorders*, 151–57. Cam-
bridge, MA: Academic Press.

Cao, J., Adam D. Galinsky, and W. Maddux. 2014. "Does Travel Truly
Broaden the Mind? Breadth of Foreign Experiences Increases
Generalized Trust." *Social Psychology and Personality Science* 5: 517–25.
https://doi.org/10.1177/1948550613514456.

Carter, Travis, and Thomas Gilovich. 2010. "The Relative Relativity
of Experiential and Material Purchases." *Journal of Personality and
Social Psychology* 98, no. 1: 146–59. https://doi.org/10.1037/a0017145.
PMID: 20053039.

Carter, Travis, and Thomas Gilovich. 2012. "I Am What I Do, Not

What I Have: The Differential Centrality of Experiential and Material Purchases to the Self." *Journal of Personality and Social Psychology* 102, no. 6: 1304–17. https://doi.org/10.1037/a0027407.

Carter, Travis, and Thomas Gilovich. 2014. "Getting the Most for the Money: The Hedonic Return on Experiential and Material Purchases." In *Consumption and Well-Being in the Material World*, edited by M. Tatzel, 49–62. https://doi.org/10.1007/978-94-007-7368-4_3.

Center for Organizational Excellence, https://center4oe.com.

Chevalier, Gaétan, Stephen T. Sinatra, James L. Oschman, Karol Sokal, and Pawel Sokal. 2012. "Earthing: Health Implications of Reconnecting the Human Body to the Earth's Surface Electrons." *Journal of Environmental and Public Health*: 291541. https://doi.org/10.1155/2012/291541.

Chikani, Vatsal, Douglas Reding, Paul Gunderson, and Catherine A. McCarty. 2005. "Vacations Improve Mental Health among Rural Women: The Wisconsin Rural Women's Health Study." *WMJ* 104, no. 6: 20-3. PMID: 16218311.

D'Amore, Louis. 1988. "Tourism: The World's Peace Industry." *Journal of Travel Research* 27, no. 1: 35–40. https://doi.org/10.1177/004728758802700107.

de Bloom, Jessica, Sabine A. E. Geurts, and Michiel A. J. Kompier. 2012. "Effects of Short Vacations, Vacation Activities and Experiences on Employee Health and Well-Being." *Stress and Health* 28, no. 4: 305–18. https://doi.org/10.1002/smi.1434.

de Bloom, Jessica., Sabine A. E. Geurts, and Michiel A. J. Kompier. 2013. "Vacation (After-)Effects on Employee Health and Well-Being, and the Role of Vacation Activities, Experiences and Sleep." *Journal of Happiness Studies* 14: 613–33. https://doi.org/10.1007/s10902-012-9345-3.

de Bloom, Jessica, Sabine A. E. Geurts, Toon W. Taris, et al. 2010. "Effects of Vacation from Work on Health and Well-Being." *Work & Stress* 24: 196–216. https://doi.org/10.1080/02678373.2010.493385.

de Bloom, Jessica, Sabine Geurts, Sabine Sonnentag, Toon W. Taris, Carolina De Weerth, and Michiel A. J. Kompier. 2011. "How Does a Vacation from Work Affect Employee Health and Well-Being?" *Psychology & Health* 26: 1606–22. https://doi.org/10.1080 /08870446.2010.546860.

de Bloom, Jessica, Michiel A. J. Kompier, Sabine Geurts, et al. 2009. "Do We Recover from Vacation?" *Journal of Occupational Health* 51: 13–25. https://doi.org/10.1539/joh.K8004.

de Bloom, Jessica, Mirjam Radstaak, and Sabine Geurts. 2014. "Vacation Effects on Behaviour, Cognition and Emotions of Compulsive and Non-compulsive Workers: Do Obsessive Workers Go 'Cold Turkey'?" *Stress and Health* 30, no. 3: 232–43. https://doi.org/10.1002 /smi.2600.

de Bloom, Jessica, Simone Ritter, Jana Kühnel, Jennifer Reinders, and Sabine Geurts. 2014. "Vacation from Work: A 'Ticket to Creativity'?" *Tourism Management* 44: 164–71. https://doi.org/

Derks, Daantje, Lieke L. ten Brummelhuis, Dino Zecic, and Arnold B. Bakker. 2012. "Switching On and Off…: Does Smartphone Use Obstruct the Possibility to Engage in Recovery Activities?" *European Journal of Work and Organizational Psychology* 23 1–11. https:// doi.org/10.1080/1359432X.2012.711013.

"Destination Healthy Aging—The Physical, Cognitive and Social Benefits of Travel." Global Coalition on Aging. https://globalcoalitiononaging.com/wp-content/uploads/2018/07/destination-healthy -aging-white-paper_final-web.pdf.

Eaker, Elaine D., Joan Pinsky, and William P. Castelli. 1992. "Myocardial Infarction and Coronary Death among Women: Psychosocial Predictors from a 20-Year Follow-up of Women in the Framingham Study." *American Journal of Epidemiology* 135: 854–64. https:// doi.org/10.1093/oxfordjournals.aje.a116381.

"Everything Tastes Different in the Air—The Effects of the Taste Experience in the Aircraft Cabin." Fraunhofer IBP, October 2011.

https://www.ibp.fraunhofer.de/en/press-media/research-in-focus/a
-feast-for-research.html.

Flaxman, Paul E., Julie Ménard, Frank W. Bond, and Gail Kinman. 2012. "Academics' Experiences of a Respite from Work: Effects of Self-Critical Perfectionism and Perseverative Cognition on Postrespite Well-Being." *Journal of Applied Psychology* 97, no. 4: 854–65. https://doi.org/10.1037/a0028055.

Fredrickson, Barbara L. 2000. "Extracting Meaning from Past Affective Experiences." *Cognition and Emotion* 14, no. 4: 577–606. https://doi.org/10.1080/026999300402808.

Fritz, Charlotte, and Sabine Sonnentag. 2006. "Recovery, Well-Being, and Performance-Related Outcomes: The Role of Workload and Vacation Experiences." *Journal of Applied Psychology* 91: 936–45. https://doi.org/10.1037/0021-9010.91.4.936.

Fuller, Patrick, Jun Lu, and Clifford B. Saper. 2008. "Differential Rescue of Light- and Food-Entrainable Circadian Rhythms." *Science* 320, no. 5879: 1074–77. https://doi.org/10.1126/science.1153277.

Gilbert, David, and Junaida Abdullah. 2002. "A Study of the Impact of the Expectation of a Holiday on an Individual's Sense of Well-Being." *Journal of Vacation Marketing* 8, no. 4: 352–61. https://doi.org/10.1177/135676670200800406.

Gilbert, David, and Junaida Abdullah. 2004. "Holidaytaking and the Sense of Well-Being." *Annals of Tourism Research* 31: 103–21. https://doi.org/10.1016/j.annals.2003.06.001.

Gilovich, Thomas, and Amit Kumar. 2015. "We'll Always Have Paris: The Hedonic Payoff from Experiential and Material Investments." In *Advances in Experimental Social Psychology*, edited by J. M. Olson and M. P. Zanna, 51:147–87. New York: Elsevier. https://doi.org/10.1016/bs.aesp.2014.10.002.

Gilovich, Thomas, Amit Kumar, and Lily Jampol. 2015. "A Wonderful Life: Experiential Consumption and the Pursuit of Happiness." *Journal of Consumer Psychology* 25: 152–65. https://doi.org/10.1016/j.jcps.2014.08.004.

Gilovich, Thomas, Amit Kumar, and Lily Jampol. 2015. "The Beach, the Bikini, and the Best Buy: Replies to Dunn and Weidman, and to Schmitt, Brakus, and Zarantonello." *Journal of Consumer Psychology* 25: 179–84. https://doi.org/10.1016/j.jcps.2014.09.002.

Gilovich, Thomas, and Victoria Husted Medvec. 1995. "The Experience of Regret: What, When, and Why." *Psychological Review* 102, no. 2: 379–95. https://doi.org/10.1037/0033-295X.102.2.379.

Godart, Frédéric, William W. Maddux, Andrew V. Shipilov, and Adam D. Galinsky. 2015. "Fashion with a Foreign Flair: Professional Experiences Abroad Facilitate the Creative Innovations of Organizations." *Academy of Management Journal* 58: 195–220. https://doi.org/10.5465/amj.2012.0575.

Greenblat, Cathy Stein, and John H. Gagnon. 1983. "Temporary Strangers: Travel and Tourism from a Sociological Perspective." *Sociological Perspectives* 26, no. 1: 89–110. https://doi.org/10.2307/1389161.

Gump, Brooks B., and Karen A. Matthews. 2000. "Are Vacations Good for Your Health? The 9-Year Mortality Experience after the Multiple Risk Factor Intervention Trial." *Psychosomatic Medicine* 62: 608–12. https://doi.org/10.1126/science.1153277.

Hartig, Terry, Ralph Catalano, Michael Ong, and Leonard Syme. 2013. "Vacation, Collective Restoration, and Mental Health in a Population." *Society and Mental Health* 3: 221–36. https://doi.org/10.1177/2156869313497718.

Hilbrecht, Margo, and Bryan Smale. 2016. "The Contribution of Paid Vacation Time to Wellbeing among Employed Canadians." *Leisure/ Loisir* 40, no. 1: 31–54. https://doi.org/10.1080/14927713.2016.1144964.

"How Long Should a Man's Vacation Be? President Taft Says Every One Should Have Three Months—What Big Employers of Labor and Men of Affairs Think on the Subject." *The New York Times*, July 31, 1910. https://www.nytimes.com/1910/07/31/archives/how-long-should-a-mans-vacation-be-president-taft-says-every-one.html.

Iwasaki, Yoshitaka. 2006. "Counteracting Stress through Leisure Coping: A Prospective Health Study." *Psychology, Health and Medicine* 11, no. 2: 209–20. https://doi.org/10.1080/13548500500155941.

Jackson, Amy Elisa. 2017. "We Just Can't Unplug: 2 in 3 Employees Report Working while on Vacation." Glassdoor, May 24, 2017. https://www.glassdoor.com/blog/vacation-realities-2017/.

"Journey to Healthy Aging: Planning for Travel in Retirement." Global Coalition of Aging, December 2013. https://www.transamericacenter.org/docs/default-source/resources/travel-survey/tcrs2013_sr_travel_and_aging.pdf.

Kahneman, Daniel, Barbara L. Fredrickson, Charles A. Schreiber, and Donald A. Redelmeier. 1993. "When More Pain Is Preferred to Less: Adding a Better End." *Psychological Science* 4, no. 6: 401–5. https://www.jstor.org/stable/40062570.

Kahneman, Daniel, Peter P. Wakker, and Rakesh Sarin. 1997. "Back to Bentham? Explorations of Experienced Utility." *The Quarterly Journal of Economics* 112, no. 2: 375–405. http://www.jstor.org/stable/2951240.

Kottler, Jeffrey A. 1997. *Travel That Can Change Your Life: How to Create a Transformative Experience.* Hoboken: Wiley.

Kottler, Jeffery A. 2003. "Transformative Travel as the Antidote for Acute Burnout and Professional Despair." *International Journal for the Advancement of Counselling* 25: 137–44. https://doi.org/10.1023/A:1026233390858.

Kühnel, Jana, and Sabine Sonnentag. 2011. "How Long Do You Benefit from Vacation? A Closer Look at the Fade-out of Vacation Effects." *Journal of Organizational Behavior* 32: 125–43. https://doi.org/10.1002/job.699.

Kumar, Amit, and Thomas Gilovich. 2015. "Some 'Thing' to Talk About? Differential Story Utility from Experiential and Material Purchases." *Personality and Social Psychology Bulletin* 41, no. 10: 1320–31. https://doi.org/10.1177/0146167215594591.

Kumar, Amit, Matthew A. Killingsworth, and Thomas Gilovich. 2014. "Waiting for Merlot: Anticipatory Consumption of Experiential and Material Purchases." *Psychological Science* 25, no. 10: 1924–31. https://doi.org/10.1177/0956797614546556.

Kwon, Jangwook, and Hoon Lee. 2020. "Why Travel Prolongs Happiness: Longitudinal Analysis Using a Latent Growth Model." *Tourism Management* 76. https://doi.org/10.1016/j.tourman.2019.06.019.

Laing, Jennifer H., and Geoffrey I. Crouch. 2009. "Lone Wolves? Isolation and Solitude within the Frontier Travel Experience." *Geografiska Annaler. Series B, Human Geography* 91, no. 4: 325–42. http://www.jstor.org/stable/40405861.

Lean, Garth L. 2009. "Transformative Travel: Inspiring Sustainability." In *Wellness and Tourism: Mind, Body, Spirit, Place*, edited by R. Bushell and P. J. Sheldon, 191–205. Teaneck, NJ: Cognizant Communication.

Lean, Garth L. 2012. "Transformative Travel: A Mobilities Perspective." *Tourist Studies* 12, no. 2: 151–72. https://doi.org/10.1177/1468797612454624.

Leung, Angela Ka-Yee, William W. Maddux, Adam D. Galinsky, and Chi-yue Chiu. 2008. "Multicultural Experience Enhances Creativity: The When and How." *American Psychologist* 63: 169–81. https://doi.org/10.1037/0003-066X.63.3.169. PMID: 18377107.

Loewenstein, George. 1987. "Anticipation and the Valuation of Delayed Consumption." *The Economic Journal* 97, no. 387: 666–84. https://doi.org/10.2307/2232929.

Lounsbury, John W., and L. L. Hoopes. 1986. "A Vacation from Work: Changes in Work and Nonwork Outcomes." *Journal of Applied Psychology* 71, no. 3: 392–401. https://doi.org/10.1037/0021-9010.71.3.392.

Maddux, William W., and Adam G. Galinsky. 2009. "Cultural Borders and Mental Barriers: The Relationship between Living Abroad and Creativity." *Journal of Personality and Social Psychology* 96, no. 5: 1047–61. https://doi.org/10.1037/a0014861.

Maddux, William W., Adam Hajo, and Adam D. Galinsky. 2010. "When in Rome...Learn Why the Romans Do What They Do: How Multicultural Learning Experiences Facilitate Creativity." *Personality and Social Psychology Bulletin* 36, no. 6: 731–41. https://doi.org/10.1177/0146167210367786.

Maye, Abewale. 2019. "No-Vacation Nation, Revised." Center for Economic and Policy Research, May 2019. https://cepr.net/images/stories/reports/no-vacation-nation-2019-05.pdf.

Merzenich, Michael M. 2013. *Soft-Wired: How the New Science of Brain Plasticity Can Change Your Life.* San Francisco: Parnassus.

Mitchell, T., and Leigh Thompson. 1994. "A Theory of Temporal Adjustments of the Evaluation of Events: Rosy Prospection and Rosy Retrospection." In *Advances in Managerial Cognition and Organizational Information-Processing*, edited by C. Stubbart, J. Porac, and J. Meindl, 85–114. Greenwich, CT: JAI Press.

Nawijn, J., and R. Veenhoven. 2013. "Happiness through Leisure." In *Positive Leisure Science*, edited by T. Freire. Dordrecht: Springer. https://doi.org/10.1007/978-94-007-5058-6_11.

Nawijn, Jeroen. 2011. "Determinants of Daily Happiness on Vacation." *Journal of Travel Research* 50, no. 5: 559–66. https://doi.org/10.1177/0047287510379164.

Nawijn, Jeroen, Jessica de Bloom, and Sabine Geurts. 2013. "Prevacation Time: Blessing or Burden?" *Leisure Sciences* 35, no. 1: 33–44. https://doi.org/10.1080/01490400.2013.739875.

Nawijn, Jeroen, M. Marchand, Ruut Veenhoven, and Ad Vingerhoets. 2010. "Vacationers Happier, but Most Not Happier after a Holiday." *Applied Research in Quality of Life* 5, no. 1: 35–47. https://doi.org/10.1007/s11482-009-9091-9. "Paid Time Off Trends in the US." US Travel Association, 2019. https://www.ustravel.org/sites/default/files/media_root/document/Paid%20Time%20Off%20Trends%20Fact%20Sheet.pdf.

Pearce, Philip L. 1981. "'Environment Shock': A Study of Tourists' Reactions to Two Tropical Islands." *Journal of Applied Social Psychology* 11, no. 3: 268–80. https://doi.org/10.1111/j.1559-1816.1981.tb00744.x.

Peltier, Dan. 2015. "4 Charts Revealing Americans' Perception of Traveling Abroad." Skift, November 10, 2015. https://skift.com/2015/11/10/4-charts-revealing-americans-perceptions-of-traveling-abroad/.

Pine, B. Joseph, and James H. Gilmore. 1998. "Welcome to the Experience Economy." *Harvard Business Review* 76: 97–105. https://hbr.org/1998/07/welcome-to-the-experience-economy.

Polk, Melody, Emily L. Smith, Ling-Rui Zhang, and Shevaun Neupert. 2020. "Thinking Ahead and Staying in the Present: Implications for Reactivity to Daily Stressors." *Personality and Individual Differences* 161: 109971. https://doi.org/10.1016/j.paid.2020.109971.

"The Power of Vacation Planning." US Travel Association, 2017. https://www.ustravel.org/sites/default/files/media_root/document/2018_Jan29_Reasearch_The%20Power%20of%20Vacation%20Planning.pdf.

Pressman, Sarah D., Karen A. Matthews, and Sheldon Cohen, et al. 2009. "Association of Enjoyable Leisure Activities with Psychological and Physical Well-Being." *Psychosomatic Medicine* 71, no. 7: 725–32. https://doi.org/10.1097/PSY.0b013e3181ad7978.

Pritchard, Annette, Nigel Morgan, and Irena Ateljevic. 2011. "Hopeful Tourism: A New Transformative Perspective." *Annals of Tourism Research* 38, no. 3: 941–63. https://doi.org/10.1016/j.annals.2011.01.004.

"Q1 2014 Employment Confidence Survey." Glassdoor, 2014. https://media.glassdoor.com/pr/press/pdf/ecsq114supplement.pdf.

Richards, Greg. 1999. "Vacations and the Quality of Life: Patterns and Structures." *Journal of Business Research* 44, no. 3: 189–98. https://doi.org/10.1016/S0148-2963(97)00200-2.

Schwartz, Barry, Andrew Ward, John Monterosso, Sonja Lyubomirsky, Katherine White, and Darrin R. Lehman. 2002. "Maximizing versus Satisficing: Happiness Is a Matter of Choice." *Journal of Personality and Social Psychology* 83, no. 5: 1178–97.

Schwartz, Tony, 2012. "More Vacation Is the Secret Sauce." *Harvard Business Review*, September 6, 2012. https://hbr.org/2012/09/more -vacation-is-the-secret-sa.html.

"SHRM/US Travel Association: Vacation's Impact on the Workplace." SHRM, November 12, 2013. https://www.shrm.org/hr-today/trends -and-forecasting/research-and-surveys/pages/shrm-us-travel -vacation-benefits.aspx.

Sonnentag, Sabine. 2012. "Psychological Detachment from Work during Leisure Time: The Benefits of Mentally Disengaging from Work." *Current Directions in Psychological Science* 21: 114–18. https:// doi.org/10.1177/0963721411434979.

Sonnentag, Sabine, and Charlotte Fritz. 2015. "Recovery from Job Stress: The Stressor–Detachment Model as an Integrative Framework." *Journal of Organizational Behavior* 36, no. 1: S76–S103. https://doi.org/10.1002/job.1924.

"The State of American Travel 2016: How Vacation Became a Casualty of Your Work Culture." US Travel Association, June 14, 2016. https://www.ustravel.org/system/files/media_root/document/PTO _SoAV%20Report_FINAL.pdf.

"State of American Vacation." US Travel Association, 2018. https:// www.ustravel.org/system/files/media_root/document/Stateof AmericanVacation2018.pdf.

Strauss-Blasche, G., Franziska Muhry, Michael Lehofer, et al. 2004. "Time Course of Well-Being after a Three-Week Resort-Based Respite from Occupational and Domestic Demands: Carry-Over, Contrast and Situation Effects." *Journal of Leisure Research* 36, no. 3: 293–309.

Tarumi, Kimio, Akihito Hagihara, and Kanehisa Morimoto. 1998. "An Investigation into the Effects of Vacations on the Health Status in Male White-Collar Workers." *Environmental Health and Preventive Medicine* 3: 23–30. https://doi.org/10.1007/BF02931235.

Transamerica Center for Retirement Studies, https://www.transamerica center.org.

Van Boven, Leaf, and Laurence Ashworth. 2007. "Looking forward, Looking Back: Anticipation Is More Evocative than Retrospection." *Journal of Experimental Psychology: General* 136, no. 2: 289–300. https://doi.org/10.1037/0096-3445.136.2.289.

Van Boven, Leaf, Margaret C. Campbell, and Thomas Gilovich. 2010. "Stigmatizing Materialism: On Stereotypes and Impressions of Materialistic and Experiential Pursuits." *Personality and Social Psychology Bulletin* 36, no. 4: 551–63. https://doi.org/10.1177/0146167210362790.

Van Boven, Leaf, and Thomas Gilovich. 2003. "To Do or to Have? That Is the Question." *Journal of Personality and Social Psychology* 85, no. 6: 1193–202. https://doi.org/10.1037/0022-3514.85.6.1193.

Westman, Mina, and Dalia Etzion. 2001. "The Impact of Vacation and Job Stress on Burnout and Absenteeism." *Psychology and Health* 16, no. 5: 95–106. https://doi.org/10.1080/08870440108405529.

Zauberman, Gal, Rebecca K. Ratner, and B. Kyu Kim. 2008. "Memories as Assets: Strategic Memory Protection in Choice over Time." *Journal of Consumer Research* 35, no. 5: 715–28. https://doi.org/10.1086/592943.

Zimmermann, Julia, and Franz J. Neyer. 2013. "Do We Become a Different Person When Hitting the Road? Personality Development of Sojourners." *Journal of Personality and Social Psychology* 105, no. 3: 515–30. https://doi.org/10.1037/a0033019.

Zinsser, William. 1997. "TRAVEL: The Road to Timbuktu: Why I Travel." *The American Scholar* 66, no. 1: 117–20. https://www.jstor.org/stable/41212596.

ACKNOWLEDGMENTS

This book was not a solo effort.

I couldn't have done it without my friends, family, and followers—the 2STRAWS tribe. I am so grateful to you for engaging with my mission, encouraging me to keep writing, and embracing me as the travel- and superfood-addicted, enlightenment-seeking, gallivanting wackadoo I am. I vow to prioritize your joy, freedom, and fulfillment in everything I create.

I must thank my team at Scribe who steered this project, including:

Jericho Westendorf and Frances Jane O'Steen, for holding me accountable.

Chas Hoppe, my pun-loving title guru.

Derek George, my masterly cover designer.

Amanda Woodard, my skilled and patient editor.

Miles Rote, for overseeing my actualization.

Alexa Davis, my marketing maven.

Special shout-outs to:

My first-semester law professor whose insufferable lecture about punctuating legal memos forced me to reconsider my entire future.

Carina Skrobecki, for the portrait on the back cover.

Calvin Gaskin, for making a cinematic book trailer with me in Uzbekistan.

The psychologists and social scientists who devote their lives to the untapped field of leisure studies.

The writers and explorers who have inspired me. Burton Holmes, inventor of the travelogue. Those ecstatic Hellenophiles, Miller and Durrell. Dharma bums and rogue rum diarists who poured it all on the page.

My judiciously unreasonable homie and sounding board, Josh Havekost, for getting it.

My parents, for teaching me how to travel and facilitating my experiential education. And for everything else.

The Universe, for listening and responding with all that I desire.

Arianne Longstocking, my love, for the merciless red swirls that brought this book to life, for guiding me into the vortex, and for living this dream with me.

We did it.

INDEX

AT&T International Day Pass, 212
Australia, 91, 104–5, 196–97
AwardWallet management tool, 66

B

backpacks, 147–48
bag choices, 142–48
Balkans, 89, 91–95
bartering, 199–200
benefits of travel
  healthy outcomes, 18–21
  memories of experiences, 28, 34, 224, 236, 242
  personal challenges, 24–26, 51, 217–21, 242
  personal transformation, 2, 28, 41–42, 240–42
bloating during air travel, 180
booking. *See* accommodations; airplane flights, booking
Booking.com, 100–101
Bose QC35 II headphones, 183
Bosnia, 91–95
boutique hotels, 101
brain, neuroplasticity of, 19–20
Branched-Chain Amino Acids (BCAA), 182
budget, travel. *See* money considerations
Businessweek, 23

C

cameras, selecting, 157–58
Camus, Albert, 24
cancellation options, 70–72, 102–3
Capital One Venture Rewards Credit Card, 166

career/work considerations, 21–24, 134–35
car rental tips, 112–16
carry-on vs. check-a-bag, 142–44
CBP (US Customs and Border Protection), 165, 167
CDWs (collision damage waivers), 112–13
Cesarine app, 121
challenges, personal, 24–26, 51, 217–21, 242
Change for Good programs, 204–5
chargers, portable, 155
Chase Freedom Unlimited card, 65
Chase Ink Business Plus card, 65, 66
Chase Ink Business Preferred card, 65, 201
Chase Sapphire Preferred, 201
Chase Sapphire Reserve, 166, 169
check-a-bag vs. carry-on, 142–44
check-in, airport, 163–68
"The Check" policy, 193–94
CLEAR security pass, 86, 167–68
clothes, packing, 141, 151–54, 189
collective restoration, 21
collision damage waivers (CDWs), 112–13
comfort zone, leaving, 17, 24–25, 50–51
communication, honest, 46–47
companions, travel, 42–49
compression socks for air travel, 176–77
Context Travel tours, 122
converters, voltage, 155–57
COVID, 139
creative innovation, 23–24
credit cards

Expedia
  as booking site, 70–72, 137
  travel studies by, 19, 22–23
expenses, travel. *See* money
  considerations
experiences, meaningful, 6, 33–38,
  39–42, 59–60, 240–42
Expert Flyer, 78

F

fasting during air travel, 181
fast passes, 125
fears about traveling, 18–26, 245–46
ferries, 107–9
first class, flying, 171
flash deals, 60
Flight 001 pouches, 149–50
flights, airplane. *See* airplane flights;
  airports, navigating
Foer, Joshua, 15
food options
  at airports, 172
  for air travel, 180–82
  discovering in destinations,
    120–22, 124–25
foreign currencies, 201–2, 204–6
foreign transaction fees, avoiding,
  201–2
France, 124–25
freedom, reclaiming, 1–2, 245–46
Freeletics fitness app, 187
free time, 126–27

G

Gagnon, John H., 25
Galinsky, Adam, 23–24
La Galleria dell'Accademia (Flor-
ence), 125
Ganges River water, 234
gift cards, points hack with, 65–66
gifts, souvenirs as, 235
Gilovich, Thomas, 33–34
Give a Day Global, 190
GivingWay, 190
Glassdoor survey, 22
Global Coalition on Aging, 20
Global Entry program, 165–67
goal-driven travel, 42, 123–24
Google Doc/Sheet as planning page,
  86–87
Google Flights, 73, 74, 85
Google Maps, 114, 216–17
Google Travel, 85, 87, 100
GPS tools, 114
Grab app, 172
Greece, 95–96, 107–9, 206, 232, 233,
  240, 243–45
Greenblat, Cathy Stein, 25
grounding (earthing), 186–87
guided tours, 122–23

H

HappyCow app, 121
hard drives for photo backups,
  228–30
hard-shell vs. softshell bags, 144–45
Hartig, Terry, 21
Harvard Business Review, 23
headphones, noise-canceling, 183
health benefits, 18–21
hedonic relativism, 33
hiking experiences, 44–45, 58
Hilton Honors American Express
  Aspire Card, 169

Lindos, Rhodes, 206
lines, waiting in, 124–25
liposomal glutathione, 177
liposomal vitamin C, 177
liquids and gels, packing, 143, 150–51
locks, luggage, 146
lodging. *See* accommodations
longevity, increasing, 20
long-flight-first rule, 69–70
LoungeBuddy app, 86, 171
lounges, airport, 168–72
luggage choices, 142–48

M

Machu Picchu, 57–59
maps, 216–17
Maputo, Mozambique, 191–93
Margarites, Crete, 194
markets, shopping in, 119–20, 191–93
Matador backpacks, 148
Matrix, ITA Flight, 74–75
meal-sharing apps, 121
meaningful travel, 6, 33–36, 39–42,
    59–60, 240–46
memories of experiences, 28, 34, 224,
    236, 242
mental health benefits, 19
metasearch tools for flight rates,
    73–75
mileage programs, 64–68, 171
mindful travel
    in airports, 174
    at destinations, 197–98
    with effort, 37
    with meaningful experiences, 6,
    33–38, 39–42, 59–60, 240–46
    vs. mindless travel, 27–28

as performance art, 35–37
by planning ahead, 5–9, 28–32
when returning home, 237–42
Mobile Passport app, 167
moisturizing, air travel and, 178–79
momentos, 231–36
Momondo flight search tool, 74
money belts, 189
money considerations
    affordability, tips for, 17–18
    with credit cards (*see* credit cards)
    with debit cards, 202
    and destination selection, 51–52,
    60
    and flash deals, 60
    foreign transaction fees, avoiding,
    201–2
    local currencies, using, 201–2,
    204–6
    priorities for, 199–201, 206–7
    tipping, 164, 202
    VAT refunds, 203–4
Moonwalking with Einstein (Foer), 15
Mostar, Bosnia, 92–94
Mozambique, 191–93
Mr. and Mrs. Smith (independent
    hotels), 101
Mumbai, India, 119–20
Musée Picasso (Antibes), 126
museums, tips for visiting, 126

N

NAC supplements, 177
National Geographic Explorer ship,
    217–21
National Geographic Traveler, 226–27
navigation apps, 216–17

mindful (*see* mindful travel)
obstacles to, 2–3, 13–18, 21–26,
245–46
risk-taking with, 16–17, 29–30, 31,
90–95
as transformative, 2, 28, 41–42,
240–42
Traveling Spoon app, 121
travel insurance, 135–37
TripAdvisor, 120
TripIt management tool, 66, 85–86,
87, 168
TripIt Pro, 66, 86, 168
tripods, 228
trips vs. vacations, 28
TSA (Transportation Security
Administration), 166
TSA luggage locks, 146
TSA PreCheck, 165–66, 168
Twelve Apostles (Australia), 196–97
2STRAWS Print Shop, 2, 157

U

UNICEF, 204–5
United Explorer Card, 166
unpacking, 238–39
US Customs and Border Protection
(CBP), 165, 167

V

vacation days, 21–24

vacation rentals, 103–5
vacations vs. trips, 28
vaccinations, 138–39
vaccine passports, 139
VAT (Value-Added Tax) refunds,
203–4
vegan/vegetarian food, 121
Verizon TravelPass, 212
visas, 139–40
vitamin D3, 177
voltage converters, 156–57
volunteer opportunities, 190
VPNs (Virtual Private Networks),
215

W

waiting in line, 124–25
water quality and consumption on
airplanes, 179, 182
weather, 52–56, 152
weddings, 95–96, 243–44
Wi-Fi. *See* internet connectivity
Wi-Fi Finder + Map, 214
Wisconsin Rural Women's Health
Study, 19
work/career considerations, 21–24,
134–35
workouts/movement, 133, 174, 176,
187–88
writing, prompts for, 230–31

CPSIA information can be obtained
at www.ICGtesting.com
Printed in the USA
FSHW021516060122
87458FS